Praise for *Smart Ass*

"Adoption — be it of a cat, a child, or in Margaret Winslow's case, a donkey — demands time, trust, and the flexibility to alter one's expectations. This tender story of a frustrated academic and an indomitable beast delivers the drama of this struggle and, ultimately, the gift of love."

— **Tina Traster,** author of *Rescuing Julia Twice* and director/producer of the documentary *Catnip Nation*

"Laugh and cry as Margaret Winslow parks her ego to accept the honest reflection a donkey provides — endearing comedy and blatant humiliation."

— **Karlene Stange, DVM,** author of *The Spiritual Nature of Animals*

"Donkeys are amazing animal beings. Twice my life was changed by an up-close-and-personal meeting with a donkey who seemed to know precisely what I was thinking and feeling. So I fully understand Margaret Winslow's being rescued by Caleb's charm, presence, and sense of humor, along with his ability to trust and to forgive. I hope *Smart Ass* enjoys a broad global audience because there are so many life lessons to be learned from the nonhuman animals who bless our lives if we allow them in."

— **Marc Bekoff, PhD,** author of *The Emotional Lives of Animals*

"I love Margaret Winslow's book and all it teaches us about the true nature of life, from the power of love to the reality of animal communication. More than anything, *Smart Ass* teaches us about reverence for life."

— **Dr. Bernie S. Siegel,** author of *Love, Animals & Miracles* and *365 Prescriptions for the Soul*

"No creatures are more misunderstood than donkeys. They challenge us to look inside ourselves for the answers to their problems, and in doing so they help us grow as humans. Every donkey will take you on a journey of self-discovery if you let them, and Caleb is no different. He has a message for you about the way we treat and respect animals, each other, and ourselves. Heartbreaking, funny, encouraging, and enlightening, *Smart Ass* is a beautifully written story that questions our own stubbornness as a species and asks us to learn how to trust ourselves."

— **Ben Hart,** animal behaviorist and trainer at
Hart's Horsemanship and the Donkey Sanctuary

"*Smart Ass* inspires us with a delightful odd-couple relationship between a white donkey and a middle-aged college professor, a grand story of humorous, wise insights into the challenges and rewards of following one's unlikely hopes and dreams. Margaret Winslow's story of Caleb the donkey unfolds as a mythic tale — wild, tender, and at times dangerous — of a woman who faces midlife issues by purchasing a stubborn, willful, and affectionate long-eared member of the equine family. Readers travel the rocky trail of their mutual life journeys, hammering out hard-won accomplishments of cross-species communication and finally arriving at a new and better way of living through loyalty to one's true self."

— **Trish Broersma,** author of *Riding into Your Mythic Life*

"*Smart Ass* is a remarkable, finely written memoir with both an engaging story and a surprising lesson. As author Margaret Winslow pursues her dream and learns to listen to her seven-hundred-pound donkey, she learns to listen to her true self. The chapters flow forward with skillfully crafted scenes, leading the reader to root for both Margaret and Caleb — and finally to share in their lifelong lesson of trust and forgiveness."

— **Susan M. Tiberghien,** author of *One Year to a Writing Life*

SMART ASS

Also by Margaret Winslow

Over My Head: Journeys in Leaky Boats
from the Strait of Magellan to Cape Horn and Beyond

The Cusp of Dreadfulness: Fifteen Seasons
in Tierra del Fuego and Patagonia

SMART ASS

How a Donkey Challenged Me
to Accept His True Nature
and Rediscover My Own

MARGARET WINSLOW

New World Library
Novato, California

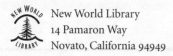

New World Library
14 Pamaron Way
Novato, California 94949

Text design by Tracy Cunningham. Typography by Tona Pearce Myers.

Library of Congress Cataloging-in-Publication Data
Names: Winslow, Margaret (Geologist), author.
Title: Smart ass : how a donkey challenged me to accept his true nature
    and rediscover my own / Margaret Winslow.
Description: Novato, California : New World Library, [2018].
Identifiers: LCCN 2018020619 (print) | LCCN 2018033116 (ebook) | ISBN
    9781608685912 (ebook) | ISBN 9781608685905 | ISBN 9781608685905
    (alk. paper) | ISBN 9781608685912 (ebook)
Subjects: LCSH: Winslow, Margaret (Geologist) | Donkeys--Training. |
    Donkeys--Anecdotes. | LCGFT: Autobiographies.
Classification: LCC SF361 (ebook) | LCC SF361 .W56 2018 (print) |
    DDC 636.1/82--dc23
LC record available at https://lccn.loc.gov/2018020619

First printing, November 2018
ISBN 978-1-60868-590-5
Ebook ISBN 978-1-60868-591-2

Printed in Canada on 100% postconsumer-waste recycled paper

New World Library is proud to be a Gold Certified Environmentally Responsible Publisher. Publisher certification awarded by Green Press Initiative. www.greenpressinitiative.org

10   9   8   7   6   5

"Yo me contento...de haber caído de mi burra, y de que me haya mostrado la experiencia la verdad."

(I am glad...to have fallen from my donkey, as that experience has shown me the truth.)

— Corchuelo in *Don Quixote de la Mancha* by Miguel de Cervantes

CONTENTS

Preface: Why a Donkey?   xi

1: The Great White Beast   1
2: The Donkey Whisperers   15
3: Smart Ass   31
4: A Donkey for Christmas   39
5: Ice Ride   47
6: Homecoming   55
7: Disaster   67
8: The Donkey Ambassador   79
9: Lead Line   85
10: Back in the Saddle   95
11: Lessons with Laura   103
12: Is This Donkey Love?   113
13: Caleb Meets the Farrier   121
14: Donkey Dressage   127
15: Donkey Gaits: Slow, Slower, and…Hold On!   133

16: Whispering to Donkeys (or Not!)   141

17: What Does a Donkey Want?   155

18: Road Warriors   161

19: Off to the Races   173

20: Mayhem in Bethlehem   185

21: The Ends of Our Tethers   195

22: Tough Love   209

23: A Donkey Speaks Up   221

24: A Reckoning   227

25: Our True Natures   235

26: An L-Back-Through into a Tight Corner   245

27: No Chickening Out   253

Postscript: Summer 2018   269

Acknowledgments   273

About the Author   277

Why a Donkey?

I COULD BE ASTRIDE A RHINO or giraffe for all the baffled stares I receive as I ride my donkey down the busy road in the suburbs of Rockland County, New York. Commuters wrench around in their seats and slam on their brakes; teenagers honk and holler.

Few in the lower Hudson valley have ever seen a donkey, outside of Shrek's sidekick and miniatures at the local petting zoo. And Caleb is no ordinary specimen. Pure white, he stands over a foot taller than the average donkey; even his ears are exceptionally long for his species. His shaggy coat completes the picture. According to small children we meet at horse shows and religious pageants, he looks like a giant Easter Bunny.

The question I invariably get from young and old alike is "What kind of horse is that?" Followed by a confused expression when I reply, "He's not a horse; he's a donkey."

The further question — "Why would you ever get one of *those*?" — is loud and clear, if often unspoken.

Good question.

As a geologist and a professor at an urban university, I found myself at a crossroads at the start of the new millennium. After thirty years of fieldwork in South America, Alaska, and the Caribbean, numerous back injuries had taken their toll. A heavy teaching schedule and administrative duties had all but doomed any opportunities to pursue new challenges in faraway places. With my oceanographer husband away at sea for months at a time and the prospect of starting a family no longer an option, I was looking for the perfect animal companion to help navigate the next phase of my life. Most people would choose a cat or dog. I chose a donkey.

I encountered donkeys for the first time in the Dominican Republic. One day during the winter of 2001, as my geology students and I collected rock samples from a riverbed, a long string of donkeys zigzagged down the steep canyon wall to join us. Each donkey carried one or two small children nestled among empty water cans. The donkeys wore no bridles or reins, so they must have known the route by heart. The kids laughed and shouted to each other as if they were perched on dusty carousel ponies, secure on their sure-footed, slow-moving mounts.

Just upstream from where we were working, the children filled the water cans while their faithful companions waited in the deep shade, snuffling greetings and nuzzling their long-eared comrades. Here I witnessed another side to their hardworking lives. Like the children, the untethered donkeys played their own versions of tag and hide-and-seek, chasing each other around trees and in and out of the river. I was enchanted, especially by their forbearance and playfulness in the face of an indifferent, even harsh, environment. At the same time, watching them made me smile. I thought that these homely cousins of horses resembled ponies — that is, ponies drawn by an enthusiastic child with a strong streak of whimsy: with the ears of a rabbit, the tail of a witch's broomstick, the stand-up mane of a punk rocker.

At that moment, a long-forgotten childhood memory sprang to mind. Every Christmas, starting at age five, I had pestered my parents to buy me the "Genuine Mexican Burro" that was advertised in the Sears catalog. The brown-and-white drawing featured a small shaggy pony-size animal with rabbit ears. The first time I turned to the page and saw the burro's huge dark eyes gazing shyly toward the viewer, I was mesmerized. I felt an intense yearning that was impossible to describe. For several years I begged my parents to get me this donkey until, finally, under the tree one Christmas morning, I found a large gray stuffed donkey. "Francis" stood watch over my dreams for years to come.

But that only partly explains why I became the owner — or should I say unwitting wrangler and straight man — of a seven-hundred-pound donkey.

When I returned home from the field in the spring of 2001, I found several donkey-and-mule organizations and magazines. According to the rapidly growing pile of books and articles I acquired, donkeys were steadfast and safe to ride. But other adjectives that experts used to describe these unshowy animals — *affectionate, playful, smart, undervalued* — struck a chord in me.

With rose-colored glasses firmly in place, I convinced myself that the side of me that had always felt underestimated as a woman in a largely male profession — the outwardly docile but tenacious striver — would resonate with a donkey's spirit. In late August 2001, I came across a small ad in the American Donkey and Mule Society's magazine, *The Brayer*, for a "large white saddle donkey."

I had no idea that a young, untrained donkey named Caleb would upend so many of my assumptions about life. Or that he would challenge me to accept his true nature — and help me rediscover my own.

 **CHAPTER 1**

The Great White Beast

THE WHITE DONKEY LOOMED over the fence, blocking out the sun. He appeared to be nearly seven feet tall.

"Oh my God. He's huge!"

I stepped back and collided with Brenda, the donkey's owner. I shouldn't have been so surprised. She had sent me a series of photos, including several where he towered over her. Had I assumed that she was a midget? "Are you sure this is the same donkey you sent pictures of?"

"Of course he is." Brenda laughed as she guided me closer to the fence. "This is Caleb."

The ad in *The Brayer* had stated that her four-and-a-half-year-old saddle donkey was 13.2 hands, or four and a half feet tall. At least on paper I understood that Caleb stood over a foot taller than a standard donkey — definitely tall enough for me to ride without my legs dangling beneath his belly. What I'd forgotten was that, as with horses, the official height is measured at the shoulder, which excludes the neck, head, and ears. In this donkey's case the ears alone were nearly a foot long. Altogether Caleb indeed blocked out almost seven feet of sunlight.

I was embarrassed to admit that I had been imagining a cuddlier creature, like the one I'd seen in the Sears catalog of my youth. Or perhaps like one of the smaller, hardworking creatures I had encountered in the Dominican Republic.

Meanwhile, Caleb pranced back and forth behind the six-foot fence, eyeing me. I leaned against the gate to get a better look at him. He loped right up and thrust his massive head over the top bar and into my chest, knocking me backward. My instincts should have told me to forget this powerful animal and back off. Instead, I stayed rooted to the spot. I was drawn to his oversize ears, his Mohawk-style mane, and, especially, his lively brown eyes. His whole stance projected curiosity and friendliness. I reached out to stroke the donkey's shaggy forehead and continued downward to the gray-and-pink freckled skin of his velvety muzzle. Beneath his chin, three-inch spikes of white whiskers tickled my hand.

I looked into his large dark eyes, thinking how much more inviting and mysterious they seemed compared with a horse's. I tried to figure out why. Was it because they were set so deeply beneath his bony brows? Or was it because his long white lashes partly veiled them? As if embarrassed by my scrutiny, Caleb lowered his head and looked away and halfway back. The lively gleam had been replaced by a soft gaze; now he appeared sad and wise.

Suddenly the donkey broke away and loped to the far side of the paddock. He stopped and looked back at me over his shoulder, his eyes sparkling with mischief. *Catch me if you can!* I was enchanted.

At the same time, cold reality pushed its way to the forefront of my thoughts: What made me think I would be able to handle such a huge, powerful animal? Now he was back at the gate, poking his muzzle through the horizontal bars. I stood there frozen, unsure what to do next.

Brenda must have sensed my indecision. "Let's go inside and have some coffee."

When I had first turned into the driveway of Brenda's small farm near Lake Erie, I had felt reassured by its tidy appearance. A new barn stood in back of a freshly painted bungalow. Inside her house, Brenda led me into a small side room where she kept a wooden loom. Skeins of rough yarn in muted, heathery shades hung in neat rows on the wall. "As I mentioned in my emails, I weave wool from my sheep and goats." She stepped over to a shelf and retrieved a small shoebox. She opened the lid and said, "Touch this. Isn't it soft?"

I stroked the grayish balls of fluffy fiber. "Is it baby alpaca?"

"No. It's Caleb's baby hair." She slowly lowered the lid and placed the box back on the shelf.

She obviously loves this donkey. So, why is she selling him?
I wondered how I could ask her.

We settled down at the kitchen table with mugs of coffee. We exchanged pleasantries about family and interests.
When I told her that my husband, Joe, had been raised
nearby, she relaxed and answered my unspoken question.

"Right now Caleb is a guard donkey for my sheep and
goats. He chases the coyotes away and herds the flock to
and from the barn. Does a real good job, too." She gazed
out the window for a long time before continuing: "But I
want him to have more of a life." She suddenly stood and
grabbed her jacket. "Let's go back out so you can get to
know him."

As soon as we stepped outside again, the donkey raced
toward us from the far side of the paddock. From where
I stood it looked as if he might launch himself in a full
frontal assault at the gate. At the last second, he planted his
hooves and skidded to a halt. He grabbed the latch with his
teeth and jiggled it, his eyes fixed on me the whole time.

Brenda leaned against the gate and opened the latch. I
suddenly panicked at the thought of getting up close to this
large beast.

"Wait! Why don't you leave him in the paddock?"
Brenda turned and stared at me, puzzled. I continued in
what I hoped was a firm professorial voice: "Let me walk
around the outside of the fence first. Watch how he moves.
You know — look at his legs?" This last part came out as a

squeak. Brenda heaved her shoulder against the gate right as the donkey lunged at it. She secured the latch just in time.

Before my visit, I had crammed as much information about judging a donkey's physical characteristics, or "conformation," as would fit on several index cards. While pretending to scrutinize the donkey's hooves, I fished the cards from my pocket. Truth be told, I hadn't digested much more than making sure that all four legs reached the ground. I scanned the first card: "Watch the donkey move. Rule out sluggishness, lameness, or asymmetry."

From outside the fence, I called out, "Come on, Caleb!" His ears immediately tuned in to my voice like antennae. He matched my pace step for step. We walked and trotted all the way to the end of the paddock and back. When the late-afternoon sun was behind him, his silhouette was surrounded by an aura of shining white hair. He looked magnificent, if a trifle silly with those king-size ears. At each turn, he tossed his head up and down and kicked his back hooves in the air with a flourish.

"Good boy! Now, whoa, Caleb." He slid to a stop directly in front of me. *How smart and eager to please he is!* I had already begun to imagine riding this donkey through the woods near my house. *He will be a perfect trail companion*, I thought.

Ten minutes later, I left Caleb rattling the gate with his nose and retreated into the house again with Brenda. It was time to discuss business. "He likes you; I can tell," she said.

While we talked, Brenda's husband walked in and said hello. Before we had a chance to introduce ourselves, he had already crossed the room to answer the ringing phone. I heard him say in a hearty voice, "No. I think it's a done deal."

My big-city skepticism reared its suspicious head. *Great. A nicely timed call from another would-be purchaser to add a little pressure to the transaction.*

Despite my attempts to appear objective and business-like, I was ready to write a check on the spot. And we three knew it. Outside, Caleb patrolled the high fence and stopped directly opposite the kitchen window. Even with the windows closed, we could hear his snuffles and grunts as he tossed his head and stared at us. When he was sure he had our attention, the grunts grew in pitch and volume to climax with a foghorn-loud, deep-throated "Hee-haw!"

Make that *four* who could tell I was hooked.

Before I wrote that check, though, I knew that I had to try riding the big donkey. There was one problem: I was a nervous rider, a *very* nervous rider. Only six months before meeting Caleb, I had broken a thirty-year hiatus and signed up for weekly riding lessons at Silver Rock Farm, a stable near my home. I had been horse-crazy as a child and started riding lessons at age nine. However, a horse had run away with me at age twenty and then stopped short, throwing me over his head. I was lucky to walk away from it with a concussion and a cracked neck vertebra, although headaches and neck pain persisted for years. As a consequence I developed an almost visceral fear of sitting atop a powerful animal, though I loved to watch horses from afar. Once I became fascinated by donkeys, pleasant memories of long-ago trail rides on horseback flooded back. An initial interest in miniature donkeys, the darlings of petting zoos, was soon replaced by research into saddle donkeys. I knew then that I'd have to overcome my fears.

Would Brenda's frisky young donkey run away with me? There was only one way to find out. "Since I want to ride him, I'd better tack him up and take him for a spin, don't you think?"

She smiled at the naive car analogy and led me back outside. I followed her as she led Caleb into the barn and tied him up. There, I touched the donkey's muscular shoulder for the first time. He felt warm and smelled of fresh hay and autumn leaves. I slowly reached up and riffled his comical, stand-up mane and was surprised by how soft it was. I had expected bristles. As I gently stroked his neck, he dropped his head and sighed.

"That means he's contented."

Me, too. "Good boy, Caleb." Brenda handed me a brush, and I mirrored her strokes as she groomed his back and sides, belly and legs. When finished with her side, she redid my feeble efforts. She then motioned for me to help her lift a massive Western saddle. We staggered across the room with it, and together we hoisted it up onto the donkey's wide back. The saddle looked ridiculous, perched as it was like a Spanish galleon on the high seas. Brenda connected the cinch around his big belly. "This is a Heiser saddle, an antique," she said. "It's worth at least $1,500. You can have it along with Caleb and all his other tack, too, for $2,000 total."

The deal kept getting sweeter and sweeter, and I wasn't even bargaining. According to Brenda, the saddle alone was worth more than the original price of the donkey. I couldn't believe my luck.

Next, she slipped the bridle over his head. Caleb pinned his ears flat and bared his big yellow teeth in a cadaverous grin. She somehow managed to pry open the big jaws and insert the bit. The maneuver looked dangerous. With his headgear buckled, Brenda led the donkey into the paddock and over to a tree stump. I mounted him, and he walked around the perimeter of the paddock, following a trajectory of his own choosing. My commands to walk, trot, turn, and stop were made after the fact. "Good boy!" I said, no matter what he did. To tell the truth, I was afraid to exercise any control in case he acted up. What if he ran away with me or collided with a tree? Two opposing thoughts battled inside my head: fear of injury and fear of revealing my incompetence in front of Caleb's owner.

On the way back to the barn, Caleb managed to wedge his enormous head between us, nudging each of us in turn with his nose. His gesture brought to mind buddies ambling home, regaling each other with their adventures. After his saddle and bridle had been removed, Brenda released him into his paddock.

Inside Brenda's sunny kitchen once more, she said, "You know you're the fifth person to look at Caleb."

"What happened to the others?"

"Oh, I rejected the previous ones because they insulted him or me," she said, crossing her arms over her chest. "Or Caleb showed dislike or fear of them."

"How did he show his dislike?" I asked. An image of trampled body parts sprang to mind.

"Oh, he 'turtled.'"

She noticed my puzzlement and explained, "He tucked his head and tail and glued himself to the spot." Her hands closed into fists. "One potential buyer kicked him. Said he was stupid."

"No!" I pictured Caleb standing there, helpless to escape the assault.

"Caleb liked you right away," Brenda said. "He's never brayed at or chased after a potential buyer before."

Okay, so maybe she was laying it on thick, but I felt pleased and even a little proud, as if I had passed some exam for worthiness. I wrote the check.

The negotiations — or lack of them — progressed smoothly. My husband, Joe, was on a research ship somewhere off the coast of Brazil, so I was free of any second-guessing on his part. He knew, of course, that I was looking for a donkey, but there was one detail I had omitted. He assumed I was still looking for a miniature donkey. I had kept the latest development in my quest — that I wanted a donkey big enough to ride — rather vague. As fate would have it, Joe had departed for his three-month "shift" at sea right before Brenda posted her ad.

Brenda wrote out a receipt and said she would hold the check pending a vet exam. And just like that, I leaped into this new relationship based on pure instinct.

Outside, my new donkey trotted back and forth head-butting the gate, his ears posed like a victory sign. I fished an apple from the car and passed it through the bars of the gate. Caleb snapped off a big chunk a half inch from my thumb. I dropped the apple and snatched my hand back. He chased the rolling apple and gobbled it up. "Goodbye, Caleb," I said. "See you soon!"

Brenda stepped up to the car window and said in a tentative voice, "One more thing: I have no right to ask, but I hope you won't change his name. Donkeys should keep their names, and we've had him since he was five months old."

"Absolutely!" I said, even though during the drive upstate I had considered renaming him "Brighty" after the brave donkey in Marguerite Henry's *Brighty of the Grand Canyon*. Caleb it would always be.

The euphoria I felt from the moment I met Caleb drained away before I reached the thruway ramp. I was flooded

Caleb at six weeks old (photo by Brenda Boyle)

Caleb at six weeks old, already catching up to Mom (photo by Brenda Boyle)

with doubts. As a fifty-year-old geology professor with a heavy teaching schedule, not to mention a bad back and a long-distance marriage, why had I just purchased a massive farm animal? An invisible noose tightened around my neck as I fought to catch my breath. I pulled over to the side of the road and practiced deep breathing until the panting subsided. *A panic attack.* I hadn't had one in years, and this was a doozy. I decided I needed to call an expert. Why hadn't I thought of this *before* I wrote the check?

Bridgman Stables, the only place in New York state that trained donkeys and mules, was only thirty miles from Brenda's. Earlier that summer, I had read their ad for donkey and mule training in an issue of *The Brayer* and had talked to Mary Lou on the phone. She had been patient with my endless questions about what she referred to with rough affection as "longears" and agreed that if I found a donkey for sale, I could send him to her for training. Brenda had told me that Caleb received a few weeks of basic training at their stable when he was three years old. Perhaps they remembered him.

A gravel-filled voice answered, "Bridgman's." I reminded Mary Lou who I was and told her that I had just purchased a donkey from Brenda Boyle. "Do you recall training a large white donkey named Caleb a year and a half ago?"

"Oh, sure, we remember Caleb very well." Mary Lou started coughing.

"Do you remember what he was like then?" I held my breath and waited. *Here it comes.*

Mary Lou said, "As I recall, he was loving and trusting."

"Oh, I am *so* glad to hear that." I sighed with relief. Before hanging up, I arranged for Caleb to be shipped to Bridgman Stables for training as soon as he passed his vet check.

Satisfied that I had made a responsible decision, I headed toward home. Despite this donkey's daunting size, I assured myself that I was accustomed to uphill battles. After all, I had taught myself to navigate boats through the uncharted regions of the Strait of Magellan, in Chile, and the Aleutian Islands of Alaska and had even backpacked across the Patagonian Andes on foot. I felt quite confident that after six weeks with donkey-and-mule specialists, Caleb would be trained and ready for his new life as my trail buddy.

Caleb watches me drive away (photo by Brenda Boyle)

CHAPTER 2

The Donkey Whisperers

ONE MONTH LATER, the events of September 11 and the destruction of the World Trade Center, only twenty-five miles away from our home, all but eclipsed any thoughts about my new donkey. While I attempted to process my own shock and fear, I'd had to reschedule several post-9/11 geology lectures at City College — not to mention attend memorial gatherings and funerals for two neighbors. How did a donkey fit into this overwhelming atmosphere of insecurity? I decided to keep my bizarre purchase to myself.

When Thanksgiving approached, I seized my first opportunity to see Caleb again. Brenda notified me that after passing his vet check, Caleb had been shipped to Bridgman Stables for training. A day or so later, Mary Lou Bridgman had left a phone message to say that he had arrived and had "settled in nicely." Her Dale Evans voice — that is, if Dale had chain-smoked — reassured me. I hadn't heard anything since.

During the three-hundred-plus-mile pre-dawn drive I thought about the challenges ahead. This was only the second time I would be face-to-face with Caleb and the first time I would meet the Bridgman family. I had paid for their six-week program in which they would review basic obedience and saddle training.

Bridgman Stables sat near the top of a long, steep road. The farm's large, multiwinged barn and other buildings nestled among brown stubbly fields bounded by wind-stripped oak and maple trees. I turned into a gravel driveway and parked in front of a small house clad in whimsically nailed-on unpainted shingles. A woman in heavy work clothes emerged from the back door. She wore a Tractor Supply baseball cap crammed down over gray curls. Her oversize stained barn coat, ancient work pants, and muck-covered rubber boots made her look like a farmworker, not the well-known "donkey whisperer" I had envisioned.

I got out and greeted her. She extended her hand to give me a lumpy handshake. "Mary Lou Bridgman," she said. "Folks call me Lou." With wrist splints stuffed inside her oversize gloves, Lou looked as if she had wrestled a number of large animals to the ground and had won most, but not all, of her battles. "Welcome to Bridgman's. Like a beer?"

I looked at my watch. *Nine in the morning?*

"Or maybe a drink?"

"Thanks. I'm fine."

We strolled into the huge barn. After my eyes adjusted to the dimness, I peered at hay and straw bales stacked up to the rafters. Dust motes drifted in and out of shafts of light from holes in the roof and fell in lazy arcs onto the straw-and-woodchip-strewn floor. A pleasant aroma of grass hay and old wood overlay the pungent smell of manure.

A faint chorus of high-pitched mule brays and horse whinnies echoed from several aisles of the barn. From a dark side aisle came a sound I had heard only once before, at Brenda's. Caleb's greeting started off with a guttural sound originating deep in his chest and progressed to rapid grunting snorts. By the time I reached his stall, the performance had rapidly crescendoed to the sound of a hundred rusty hinges wrenched open at once, culminating in a county-saturating blast of a tractor trailer's stuck air horn.

"I'm coming, Caleb!" I called in my heartiest voice. I felt giddy with joy.

Foot-long white ears sprouted over the wooden gate of a stall. As I reached up to stroke his shaggy winter fur, I was horrified: Caleb had grown to the size of an elephant, a white elephant, at that. How was that possible? Some of my fear about his apparent growth spurt dissolved when I noticed that the stall floor lay several inches higher than the aisle. Once I recovered from the initial shock, I felt a strange mix of elation and trepidation at the sight of him. Although I hadn't done this before, I reached over the high wall and hugged his neck. His freckled nose snuffled my hair. It felt so good to be far from the ongoing turmoil in New York City and near this warm animal.

With halter and lead line in hand, I opened the gate latch. Like a bronco released from the chute at the rodeo, Caleb charged right past me and trotted out into the aisle. Lou doffed her cap and whacked him twice on the nose. "Back!" she growled. He backed into the darkest corner of his stall, eyes averted. "Don't let him think he can run over you."

"Okay," I said, unsure how to prevent it. Lou caught my hesitation and stepped inside, slid the halter over Caleb's nose and ears, and clipped on the lead line, all in one smooth move. She handed the rope to me. As soon as we exited the stall, the four-legged leviathan towed me down the aisle toward the exit. Lou grabbed the rope to stop us.

"Don't let him drag you around like that. Make him walk at your pace, not his."

Easier said than done, I thought. I grasped the rope and stepped forward, but the donkey had planted his hooves and refused to budge. I turned toward him, leaned back with my full weight against the line, and said in a soft voice, "Let's go, Caleb. Please."

Lou stood with her hands on her hips. "You'll never win a tug-of-war with a donkey. Face forward and say 'Walk on!' like you mean it!" She looked at the floor, slowly shaking her head. "When you turn to look at him, he thinks you want to stop or go in the direction you're *facing*."

"Oh, okay. That makes sense."

At the sound of Lou's command, "Walk on!" Caleb burst into a spirited trot only to stop again after a few yards. I ran around to his rear and pushed against his stiff rump. With yanks and shoves, I more or less guided the donkey toward a brightly lit room.

Lou said, "Oh, by the way, don't talk so much around Caleb, except to use the key commands you're teaching him. Otherwise your words will mean gobbledygook to him and he won't listen to anything."

Her advice disappointed me. One of my unspoken fantasies involved Caleb and me ambling into the sunset, his long ears turned toward me as I shared my hopes and secrets. Aware that I was channeling Francis, the stuffed donkey of my early girlhood, I shook off the childish dream.

In the bright light of the grooming station, I saw that Caleb's thick winter pelt had transformed him from the fairly sleek donkey I had met at Brenda's into a giant furry white rabbit. His hair, three or four inches in length, was much longer and coarser than winter coats I had seen on most horses, which further explained his increase in size. Even his ears were covered and lined with thick white hair. I couldn't resist rubbing my nose into his neck and breathing in the spicy smell of hay and warm animal. He tilted his head toward me and rubbed it against my ear. My heart swelled with affection. "I'm so glad to be here with you, buddy." Any remaining tensions of the last several weeks in the city vanished.

At Lou's urging, I pushed the stiff brushes through

his muddy, matted fur. After forty-five minutes my arms ached, but Caleb's coat gleamed whiter than I believed possible from brushing alone. Lou explained, "Every time you groom Caleb, pretend he's going to the Olympics. Being well groomed gives dignity to the animal. Donkeys have been neglected, underrated for centuries. They deserve the same care as horses."

In a large tack room at the other end of the barn, I strained to lift the leaden Heiser saddle I had purchased with Caleb. On the way back, I passed a grizzled old prospector swinging pitchforks of clean straw into a stall. Smiling through a full beard, he introduced himself: "Jack Bridgman, Lou's husband. Or I should say barn slave." I nodded hello but continued my stiff-legged shuffle, afraid my arms would be wrenched from their sockets before I reached the grooming station.

Jack and (Mary) Lou Bridgman (photo by Joe Stennett)

He called after me: "Come over for a drink when you're finished."

When I finished my lesson and untacked Caleb, it would still be only 11 AM. Rather early for me to imbibe, but maybe today marked a special occasion. "Thanks," I said.

When I reached Caleb's side, I swung the saddle around like a discus thrower and scraped the donkey's flank with a stirrup before dropping it. Lou bent down and swept it up and onto the donkey's back. "There," she said. *Easy for her, maybe.*

I was reaching under his bulging belly to grab the cinch when Lou called out, "Careful of his hind legs!" I straightened up like a shot. Standing before me was an inert white mass. "See how his ears are pinned back? And one hind hoof is pointed, tapping the floor? His hip and leg are tensed and ready to kick out."

"I think I see it." I needed to learn how to read Caleb's body language, and fast. In the absence of further directions, I stroked his head and whispered his name, until his ears popped back up. He dropped his head a little and let out a long sigh of contentment. It seemed like I should sigh, too, so I did.

Lou said, "Okay, now you can do it."

I ducked beneath his furry belly, grabbed the girth, and inserted it into the buckle.

Lou watched as I attempted to guide Caleb up a long

slope toward the big indoor ring, stopping us several times. "Halt. He's crowding you. Turn him around. Come on back down the ramp." We started over. And again. In my anxiety to accomplish what suddenly seemed to be an impossible task, I started to pull and jerk on the rope.

"Stop yanking on the rope! Stop acting like you're in a big rush."

I dropped the rope and stared at her. I thought we were late for the lesson.

"Make him think you have all day," she explained. "If you're in a hurry, a donkey will *take* all day."

I picked up the rope and applied light pressure. "Please, Caleb, please move," I whispered to him. The ring now seemed to be as unattainable a destination as the summit of Everest. Less than halfway up the slope, the donkey slammed on the brakes again. Despite my pleas, Caleb leaned back on his heels and stayed put.

"Act like you have one clear purpose," Lou called from the bottom of the incline. "Visualize in your head where you want him to go."

At the sound of Lou's deep voice, some switch in the donkey's fuzzy brain changed from *stop* to *go*, and he trotted up the ramp, towing me behind like a one-armed water-skier. At the doorway to the ring, he planted his feet again and I collided with his furry rump.

Caleb's ears were tuned toward the voice of a young woman inside the ring who was calling out sharp commands to a class of young riders. Lou introduced me to her daughter, Farley. The tall, slim woman in jeans and a battered cowboy hat looked Caleb and me over before loping to a far corner of the ring.

I looked around the large indoor arena. A dull autumn light filtered through clear plastic insets in the roof, illuminating a sandy track with plastic barrels, traffic cones, and ramps scattered around the central area. One preteen after another cantered around the perimeter, each riding a sleek dark brown mule. Except for the elongated ears, legacies of their donkey sires, these donkey-horse hybrids resembled their Thoroughbred mothers. At the end of their lesson, the girls dismounted and walked their obedient mules out the door. I told myself that under Lou's gruff tutelage, in a few weeks I would be riding and handling my donkey with as much confidence as those girls.

"Mount up over there," Lou said and left me to it. Her voice had taken on a businesslike tone, much like her daughter's. Without Lou's step-by-step instructions, I suddenly felt exposed. I always did poorly when faced with critical scrutiny. Holding the very end of the rope, I stretched it and my arms until I could almost, but not quite, reach the mounting block. Instead, I hooked it with the toe of my boot and inched it over to Caleb's side. "Like bringing the mountain to Mohammed," I mumbled at him. Caleb stared at the far wall, unconcerned. I climbed the steps, but before I could swing a leg over, he lurched forward. I hopped off the block, moved it, and tried again. Same thing. After a third aborted attempt, Lou came over and held Caleb's head while I climbed aboard.

With reins in hand, I tapped his side and whispered, "Walk on."

Caleb traced the perimeter of the ring at a brisk walk. I began to relax. *I'm riding my own donkey! This isn't so hard!* As if he could read my mind, he tossed his head, wrenching the reins from my grasp, and trotted straight for a wall. I collected the reins and yelled, "Stop!" I torqued his head away from the wall, but this merely drew his rear quarters and my knee even closer. I cried out when my shin caught a piece of loose molding.

Lou turned away from her conversation with Farley. "Here, let me show you something." She walked up and grabbed Caleb's bridle. "When he tries to scrape you off on the wall, turn his head *toward* the wall, like this. Let him scrape his nose on it. He'll move off pretty smart."

I kicked Caleb on the flanks and said, "Walk on." Gripping the right rein with both hands, I hauled his granite skull toward the wall. As soon as his nose rubbed the wall, he moved off and veered toward the track. *It worked!*

He didn't follow the outer track for long, though. As soon as Lou turned her back, Caleb jerked the reins from my grip again and headed straight for a jump in the middle of the ring. There, he jolted to a full stop, catapulting me between his ears. I grabbed the saddle just in time. In an attempt to back him up, I tugged first on one rein then the other. He wouldn't budge. Meanwhile, Farley's students had returned and added to the audience of astonished observers.

Lou sauntered over. People who work around large animals, I noticed, move slowly, their arms at their sides. They keep their gaze down and a bit off to the side as they approach the animal. No sudden movements. Perhaps a beer before lunch contributes to their serene approach.

"You know, Caleb's trying to scare you into giving up. And it's working, right?"

I hung my head, ashamed.

"Okay, whip and kick him forward. Call his bluff. He wants to crash his front legs into the support beam? Let him."

Now she's asking me to call his bluff. How was I supposed to know what was hidden inside his hoary brain? I kicked and said, "Walk on," and, miracle of miracles, he backed up. Was this another example of reverse psychology?

Lou reinforced her earlier advice about talking too much: "Remember, don't use more than one phrase for the same command. 'Whoa,' 'Oh,' and 'No' all sound alike to him."

In my nervousness I had already spouted a full thesaurus of synonyms and unrelated words like *Stop, Quit, Stay, Shit, Damn it, Ouch, Sorry,* and *Oh no!*

In less than two hours, I already felt overwhelmed, not

so much from the deluge of new information but from the strange training methods. Much was expected but little explained. Lou's and Farley's silence could be interpreted several ways. Perhaps they expected the rider and donkey to figure things out on their own. Or perhaps they saw a hopeless case, not worth their time, and were waiting for me to recognize the folly of my feeble efforts. And give up.

Caleb declared the lesson over by trotting out the open door. Outside his stall, I dismounted. Once I stowed him and his gear away, forgoing the drink with Jack, I headed east toward the only coffee shop in the faded village of Warsaw, New York. While I waited for my sandwich order, I opened the notebook I had started months before I met Caleb. According to an article from The Donkey Sanctuary in Sidmouth, England, I was to "ignore unwanted behavior and reward positive steps effusively." Intimidation worked with horses but not donkeys, it warned.

Intimidation had never worked with me, either. It made me curl up inside myself, deaf both to the criticism and, unfortunately, to the object of the lesson. As the first — and only — woman in most of my geology courses in college, I had chafed under subtler forms of bullying and intimidation. Patronizing remarks like "Are you sure you can keep up?" barely concealed my professors' contempt.

The waitress plunked a tray with food and silverware on the table and left me to my ruminations. Finally, I identified what was bothering me. So far, the Bridgman method, at least Farley's, demonstrated the exact opposite of positive reinforcement.

My thoughts drifted back to my donkey. After he had been wrenched from the only home he had known since he was a foal, his life now consisted of long hours pent up in a dark stall. His loneliness was relieved only by one-hour lessons during which everybody, including me, yelled at him. Did he think that his present circumstances represented his entire future life? And, if so, did that explain his resistance? Seen in this light, his mischief in the ring might be his only means of protecting his spirit. A flood of sympathy brought tears to my eyes.

But the fact was, the Bridgmans were the *only* donkey trainers I knew of in the Northeast, and they had decades of experience with donkeys. I was here to learn, not debate methods.

I paid the check and drove up the steep hill on the east side of town and into the driveway of a cinderblock motel. Outside the office a brutal northwesterly wind swooped across fields of dried grasses that stretched in all directions. According to my road map, Attica prison lay only eight miles north. An image of Caleb's present accommodations came to mind.

The rest of the weekend lessons followed the same dismal routine. I groomed and tacked my donkey under Lou's close supervision, but in the ring, her intense scrutiny abruptly ceased. Lou and Farley merely watched me — lit cigarettes dangling from their lips, arms crossed, with beers in hand — as I scraped more paint off the walls; lurched over ramps sideways curled into a fetal position; and huffed, cussed, and pleaded for help. As we wobbled past, Farley and her mom muttered cryptic comments to each other.

"Noodle arms."

"She's a wiggle worm in the saddle."

"Absolutely no clue."

My heart sank in agreement.

At the end of my last lesson, after returning Caleb to his stall, I came back to the ring, where Lou and her daughter stood conferring quietly in the doorway. I asked them, "So, how am I doing?"

Farley wasted no time before snapping, "What I want to know is this: Which do you want, an obedient riding animal or a spoiled pet?"

"Well." I hesitated, stunned by her tone of voice. "How about a well-behaved pet I can ride?"

Farley snorted her reaction at Lou and stalked off.

As I started the long drive back to New York City for another month of classes, I considered my situation. Caleb may have made an ass out of me in front of the Bridgmans, but there was still time for them to work their magic. Compared with breaking into the all-male world of field geology in the 1970s, training a donkey with the help of experts should be a cinch. Nevertheless, a worry niggled at the back of my mind: Caleb and I formed an unequal partnership from the beginning, with one member of the team a lot stronger and — I suspected — a lot more willful than the other. Yet, I convinced myself that by the time I returned in mid-December for my final two weeks of training, I'd have a slew of stories about how the smart ass trained the dumb ass.

It wasn't clear to me yet which role I would be playing.

CHAPTER 3

Smart Ass

THE WEEK BEFORE CHRISTMAS, I loaded up my car for the long drive north to Bridgman Stables.

During the drive I mused on the timing of this impulsive acquisition. It could hardly have been worse. The college administration had lately been threatening a change toward an "entrepreneurial model." The plans had nothing to do with enhancing the educational experience of students or faculty, and everything to do with the provost's nefarious proposal to rent out classrooms and offices to commercial interests.

Twenty years earlier, I had chosen to teach at City College because undergraduate education came first. From day one, I loved teaching my urban students about the wonders of the natural world, and my efforts had won praise and prizes. Those skills, sadly, now seemed irrelevant. I turned my thoughts to my latest educational challenge: training Caleb. I relaxed my shoulders and smiled. After thirty years of teaching sometimes-difficult students in several countries, it should be a snap.

On the last twenty miles of the drive, heavy snow overwhelmed the windshield wipers and I nearly missed the turnoff to the stable. Lou met me at the barn door and gathered me into a warm bear hug. "How was the drive?"

Imitating the family's laconic tone, I shrugged like the tough cowgirl I would never be: "No problem, really. Bit of snow." In truth, I was a very fearful driver in snow and dreaded the drive to the motel.

She knew from my previous visit that I would decline a morning libation, so she waved toward the aisle, where loud, snuffling groans guided me to Caleb's stall. "Hi, Caleb. I'm glad to see you, too!" His enthusiasm instantly erased the tensions of the long winter drive. Inside the stall's dark confines, the donkey shoved his head to my chest until I was squashed against the wall. With feeble pats and pleas, I extracted the big beast from his stall.

I groomed and tacked him without Lou's corrections and somehow — by offering frequent portions of baby carrots and begging — wrestled him up to the ring. Weak winter rays filtered through the snow-covered skylights; the few electric lights barely pierced the gloom. Lou and Farley were bundled up in barn coats, wool caps, and scarves. Our breath condensed in the cold air, but at least we were protected from the wind that rattled the steel building.

After I had mounted (only three attempts this time),

Caleb trotted straight for a wall, stopped short, and stared at it. As if to underscore my ineptitude, a kindergartener, whom I'd heard Farley call Crystal, cantered past on a huge mule, her satiny blouse and pink cowboy hat passing in a blur.

Farley shouted at me, "Whip him! Don't let him do that to you!"

Right from the get-go, I struggled under the Bridgmans' critical gaze. I tapped the donkey's flank gently until Lou's and Farley's shouts of "Whip him! Kick him! Harder!" shamed me into action. In response to increasingly frenzied blows to his flanks and neck, Caleb tucked his tail and, with a loud sigh, dropped his nose to the ground. His front legs began to buckle, tilting me onto his neck.

Lou called out, "He's going to roll on you! Pull his head up and kick him, hard."

It took all my strength to lift what felt like a hundred pounds of donkey head. I swung the whip again. Caleb's flanks flinched from the blows, but he remained rooted to the spot, head down, the poster child of an abused animal. What Brenda had called "turtling." Then and there, I turtled right along with him.

Farley stomped over with a six-foot-long whip. Caleb's head popped up, and he sidestepped toward the track. "He was coming along *just fine* all month," she said. "Even the kids rode him."

I found that hard to believe but didn't say so. Before

she resumed her spot near the wall, Farley added, "Margie, you've got to decide who is alpha right from the start."

That decision had been made long before, the moment he first sized me up from behind the fence at Brenda's. In truth, despite the four diplomas from Columbia University displayed on my office wall, I had never been capable of carrying off the alpha pose. And Caleb, I suspected, could see right through me.

The rest of the lesson was equally grim. Certain that Lou and Farley blamed me for Caleb's misbehavior, I plodded on, whispering praise, pleas, and curses to the tufted knob between the donkey's ears. Lou repeated for the tenth time, "Don't praise him until *after* he has done the whole lesson, and has done it correctly." After what seemed like an eternity, I interpreted the rapidly fading light and the instructors' rapidly fading interest to mean the lesson was over. I swung a leg over, wobbled, and slid to the floor.

Farley took the reins and mounted. To my surprise, Caleb twisted his tender mouth and jaw to resist her attempts to pull him away from the exit. In the end, a heavy application of whip and spurs did the trick. He set off around the ring at a brisk trot. After one perfect circuit, she dismounted and handed me the reins. "There. See?"

Well, I saw two different things: Farley's muscles, whip, and spurs overcame Caleb's resistance at the end, but she had waged a mighty battle to subdue him. I wiped my sweaty hands on my pants and sidled up to the dim corner where

Farley and Lou now huddled. Speaking to the ground, I said, "I'm trying to be tough with him —"

"Hell, you're singing 'Caleb, Caleb' the minute you leave your car," interrupted Farley, "and then he brays enough to wake the whole county." Meaning the Bridgmans and their mules and dogs, since I never saw another soul in this corner of Wyoming County. I fumed in silence as we left the ring. On the way, Caleb snatched a mouthful of hay from a tall stack of bales, nearly toppling it. I jerked him away before anyone noticed and nudged the bale back into place with my boot.

Farley wasn't finished with me. "You keep praising him just because he's your donkey. He gets a carrot for doing nothing — before he's even gotten out of his stall."

As much as I bristled at her tone, Farley was right: I confused bribes with rewards. I bribed Caleb from the minute I arrived, begging him to behave, making bargains regarding future behavior that the donkey couldn't understand. I kicked at the hay bale. "Maybe he needs a smarter owner."

"Come on, now." Lou smiled as she exhaled a thin stream of smoke into the cold air. She patted my arm. "He's just pushing your buttons."

Jack appeared from around the corner, pushing a wheelbarrow full of manure. "You know what I call donkeys?" he said with a twinkle in his eye.

"No, what?" At that point I was game for a joke.

"Horses with brains." He paused to gauge my reaction. "They're damned smart. Yesiree. Damn smart." His laugh was a wheezy chortle.

Jack's remark reminded me of my only joke about donkeys, so I piped up and said, "Do you know why they don't send donkeys to college?"

"No. Why?" Jack asked.

"Because nobody loves a smart ass."

Jack and Lou looked at each other. A signal passed between them before they laughed.

"Pretty funny, coming from a college prof," Jack said.

This was the first time anyone here had acknowledged that, away from this farm, I had a respectable job — that maybe I was something other than a hopeless fool.

"Another thing about donkeys," Lou said. "They ought to be born at age eight or nine. Until then you can train them all you want, but it won't stick. They mature slower than horses, you see."

"Now you tell me." I was absolutely certain that neither Lou nor Brenda had mentioned this tiny fact.

Lou whispered in Jack's ear. "Caleb's only four and a half?" he asked. "No wonder. Just a baby. Got a long way to go, yet."

I looked at my big hairy baby and laughed. He instantly picked up on my lightened mood. All the way back to his stall, he trotted along, playfully nipping my forearm. "I'm glad at least *somebody* had fun," I said to his eagerly twitching ears. He stretched his neck over the hastily locked gate and smeared hay-flecked snot across my chest. "Caleb," I whispered, "you have to help me out here." Surely those deep-set brown eyes understood how important our journey together was. But just to let him know we were still friends, I gave him a carrot.

During the next week, my whole existence shrank to humiliating lessons under the watchful eyes of the Bridgmans and their students. I'm not sure which I dreaded more: the drive to and from the stable in the ice and snow or the certainty of disaster during the lesson. Back at the college, I saw myself as a competent teacher and guide in the classroom and the field. Under the Bridgmans' scrutiny, however, I felt reduced to a struggling student for the first time since graduate school. As a teacher, I strove to explain the rationale behind each assignment. But there was no sign of that here. Perhaps they assumed everyone knew from birth how to handle donkeys. I imagined Farley's way of putting it: "Anyone with half an ounce of common sense oughta know…" But I had never had a student as challenging as this donkey, nor had I ever felt so helpless.

CHAPTER 4

A Donkey for Christmas

OTHER THAN THE THICK SNOW on the ground, there was no other sign that it was Christmas Eve. I was far from home, and I wasn't the only one. At that moment, Joe's ship was mapping the ocean floor off the coast of Australia. The day before I had finally found a library that was actually open and had internet access. *Hallelujah.* I sent Joe a brief, upbeat email but had no idea when he would get it or reply.

While I stowed the saddle and bridle, I made a valiant attempt to stave off the blues by singing Christmas carols. It wasn't working.

Lou walked past the tack room and lingered for a while. "Come on over for a drink when you're finished here," she said.

Aside from quick sprints to use the Bridgmans' bathroom and helping myself to coffee or hot water for tea, I hadn't been inside their home. In fact, until Caleb woke the family up with his blasted greetings and I caught hell for it,

I had believed that the building was a tack room or office, and that the family lived elsewhere.

When I entered Lou's kitchen, she had already put the kettle on to boil. With a cup of tea in hand, I followed her through a dim hallway and stopped to examine a dusty display of medieval-looking iron bits, chains, and straps — accessories deemed necessary for the successful control of donkeys and mules. Included among the options were some thick double-chain mouthpieces that looked intimidating enough to control an elephant. Did longears require all that stuff? Surely not *my* donkey.

I caught up with Lou in what I assumed was the living room, a large, empty space lined with the same bare, unsanded wood planks on the walls as on the floor. Jack sat in a wooden rocking chair flanking a woodstove, sipping his drink. Lou joined him on another chair near the stove. Farley arrived, beer in hand, and took her seat on the hard bench next to me. I was sure they thought I was a teetotaler by then, as I had consistently turned down their offers of morning picker-uppers. So, when I lifted the bottle of Kentucky's finest from my day pack, Lou and Jack smiled and held out their glasses. Farley declined, so I poured a drop of bourbon into my teacup.

After we wished each other Merry Christmas, Jack and Lou talked quietly about farm business. When the topic veered toward donkeys or their training, I said, "I've read that…" or "Is that true?" I wondered if the Bridgmans spent their free time talking about donkeys, or whether my single-minded prompting had steered the conversation toward them.

Meanwhile Farley continued sitting by my side on the hard bench, saying nothing. The wind shrieked around the house and I shivered, too far from the woodstove to feel any heat, except for a warm flush that spread through my chest from the hot bourbon. I looked around the spare room for holiday inspiration. A couple of red-and-green greeting cards piled on an end table next to Lou were the only signs of Christmas for this hardworking bunch. No TV, no radio. I got up to stretch my back and to get nearer to the stove, and peered at the framed pictures on the walls. The whole family was represented, all holding ribbons and trophies as they posed with their steeds. A youthful Jack sat on a Tennessee walking horse in the special saddle, set far back on the horse's kidneys. In his prime, the grizzled old manure slinger must have been a serious showman as well as a trainer. Other photos showed Lou in spangled Western finery, a blonde Dale Evans, holding ribbons next to her sleek palomino. On the opposite wall Farley stood at attention in a black velvet helmet and jodhpurs, a rack of blue ribbons in one hand, the reins of a tall brown mule in the other.

I felt awkward sitting next to the bored or resentful Farley, who merely mumbled answers to my queries — if she bothered to answer at all. I mused about her coolness, which I assumed was based on my utter incompetence with Caleb. I began to notice, though, that her sullenness also extended to her parents, whom I overheard offering her obviously unwanted advice regarding her training methods. Her impatient, dismissive rejoinders reminded me more of a teenager than a thirty-year-old woman.

When I returned to the bench, the room fell silent except for the pop and hiss of logs in the stove. I wiggled on the cold wood, attempting to ease my aching back. Not only was it sore from the donkey's torquing me around in my daily struggles to groom and ride him but also from the sagging bed in the cheap motel I returned to every night.

The Bridgmans carried on discussing their business. They were obviously devoted to training longears, for they spoke of them with gruff affection. I wondered: Did this mean that they were perverse masochists? Or had they glimpsed reflections of themselves mirrored in their donkeys' misbehavior — as untamable outlaws or underdogs? I realized, with a jolt, that this had once applied to me, too — the tomboy explorer of my childhood, and the college student who persisted in studying geology despite barriers to women. When had I become such a conciliatory, conflict-adverse wimp of a college professor who shrank from controversy? What had happened to the bold outlaw in me?

Well, maybe not all was lost. After all, I had gone out and bought myself a donkey.

As if Jack could read my thoughts, he asked, "Why did

you buy a donkey, anyway?" The awkwardness and abruptness of his question yanked me out of my brooding. The Bridgmans had probably been speculating about this at some length. The question could be interpreted several ways: *Why a donkey instead of a horse? Why a donkey instead of, say, some other impulsive midlife purchase like a sports car or sailboat? Why me, a middle-aged, obviously clueless rider?*

"I loved donkeys from the first moment I discovered an ad for a 'Genuine Mexican Burro' in the Sears catalog." I was about to launch into a charming Christmas story about my childhood obsession, when I noticed that everyone was staring at the floor. Time to regroup. I ventured into what I hoped was a more reasonable explanation: "I first encountered donkeys when I worked in the Dominican Republic. Downtrodden but playful. To me they looked like horses with low self-esteem…" Even that story sounded naive at best, if not delusional. My voice trailed off to nothing.

Lou broke the silence. "I'm going to fetch some refills. How about you, Margie?" I raised my cup, grateful.

She returned with a steaming cup of tea and offered me a choice between it and the bottle of bourbon she'd lifted from the side table. I accepted the half-filled teacup but held it up and nodded at the bottle. Lou filled the cup to the brim and topped up everyone else's drinks.

She finally interrupted the uncomfortable lull: "You know, Caleb weighs close to seven hundred pounds. If you want him to do anything, even just to move him from a paddock to his stall, you must establish control." The alpha thing again.

My head swirled with conflicting thoughts: Did I want to have Caleb obey me? Well, yes — up to a point. Could I force him to follow my instructions? Possibly. But did I want to use force? I shook my head as if answering myself.

"But more than anything," Lou said, "before a donkey will submit, he needs to *trust* you."

Jack picked up the theme: "That's right. He needs to trust that you know what you're doing, that your commands are reasonable and safe."

Even Farley agreed. She said, "The commands, most of all, must be consistent."

My head filled with images of jerking reins, wobbling posture, and random yelling, and I felt a sudden wave of discouragement. I looked out the window, where the dark silhouettes of trees whipped back and forth in the wind. *What am I doing here?* Here I sat, far from friends and loved ones, in a godforsaken frozen hell, trying to gain the approval of a crusty bunch of mule skinners. And what sort of people lived in unheated, unfinished houses in this no-man's-land with a bunch of mules, anyway? *The kind who quaff bourbon for breakfast, that's who!* Struggling year after year with intransigent longears would drive anyone to drink. I gulped my laced tea and coughed from its bite.

Lou tapped her cigarette against an overfilled metal ashtray. Perhaps picking up on my disillusionment, she said, "You know, Caleb is just testing you, figuring out where you fit into his family group."

Family. Besides my globe-trotting husband, my family consisted only of a sister and three very dear friends, all of whom lived far away. *Would Caleb and I ever become a family? And what would a donkey's family look like?* So far, all I knew was that wild donkeys live semisolitary lives yet seek out and enjoy company and novel experiences. It sounded rather uncomfortably close to home.

Jack's words pulled me from my reverie. He picked up on Lou's main point, which I had forgotten: "Oh yeah. Donkeys and mules just love to test you."

"Okay, so are you telling me that Caleb knows exactly what I want him to do but is thwarting my efforts *on purpose?*"

"Sure looks like it, sometimes."

"But, why?"

Lou and Jack looked at each other and shrugged. Jack offered, "Because he's a *donkey*." They broke out laughing. I felt a vast sense of release from my chronic feeling of inadequacy. I joined them in a toast: "To longears!"

CHAPTER 5

Ice Ride

WEDNESDAYS WERE REST DAYS at the barn. Over breakfast at the café, I thought about how I might occupy myself on a dull winter's day after Christmas. My thoughts drifted back to my rabbit-eared friend. How would he spend his day off?

Worried that the roads would soon be too slick to venture out of town, I hurried to my car. On the way, an idea came to me: *we could do a trail ride!* Though the snow was too deep for a hike — for a two-footed animal, that is — Caleb could handle it easily. After all, my dream had been to explore woodland trails together. There was one potential snag: according to the training contract, I could ride only during lessons. But surely they would grant me an exception.

On the last hill before the stable, a stab of anxiety pushed the pleasant anticipation away. Up until this point, I had ridden Caleb only when a trainer was present. It was only too obvious that the presence of any of the Bridgmans had a sobering effect on Caleb. Despite all the assurances from books that donkeys don't buck or bolt, my biggest fear, since that riding accident so long ago, was that I would be thrown off. Deep snow, however, meant a slower ride and, if I did fall off, a soft landing. I vacillated between confidence and worry as I drove.

I visualized the layout of the stable. Deep, unpacked snow covered most of the thirty-acre farm. The sloping hillside that extended from the parking area up to the woods was underlain by grass, I recalled from Thanksgiving, and most of the perimeter was fenced in. There were no rocks or stumps to stumble over. The pleasant image of a snowy ride returned.

I was jolted from my reverie when my car slalomed across a skating-rink-size expanse of ice that used to be the parking area. The car stopped only when it fetched up against a snowbank. I slipped carefully from the driver's seat and, by holding on to the car, inched around to the back.

Time to rethink the plan. From where I stood, it looked like only the parking area was covered in ice. The lower entrances to the barn and to the house looked iffy: chunks of broken snow and ice glinted in the sun. I extended my gaze along the near side of the barn complex as it sprawled uphill. The middle door faced untouched snow, and the upper entrance, the one that exited the ring, was hemmed in by deeper snow. I could guide Caleb straight from the sandy ring right into knee-deep snow. *Perfect.*

Still, I sought Lou's permission. I skated toward their back door and stepped into the dark vestibule. Farley was pulling on her rubber boots, so I asked her instead. "Do you think it's okay if I take Caleb out for a ride in the snow today?"

"Up to you," she said. She shrugged into a heavy coat and stepped past me. I took her flat response to mean that the conditions were safe enough for a rider with my limited skills on a semitrained animal.

Caleb's deep honk greeted me as soon as I entered the gloomy barn. At his stall, he grabbed the collar of my parka and shook me like a dog shakes a toy. "Okay, Caleb, I'm here. Settle down." I pried the soggy layers of my jacket from his mouth. As soon as I opened the stall door, he bolted, heading straight for the grooming area. "Good boy, Caleb." I hastened to catch up and put his halter and lead on in case Farley rounded a corner.

Thanks to Caleb's atypical cooperation at the grooming station, I brushed, tacked, and mounted him in record time. I aimed him toward the ring and chased him up the ramp.

"Trying to leave without me?" I asked him. I grabbed the reins and mounted. Too bad no one witnessed my flawless mount. Caleb stopped at the exit, presumably to let his eyes adjust to the glare. He stepped carefully, raising one leg and then another before putting his full weight on it. He was testing his footing. "Smart donkey!" I patted him.

One hoof at a time, we eased out into the field. Halfway up the hill, Caleb's dainty hooves punctured a thick crust of ice, revealing a foot of soft snow underneath. Now he was forced to lift his legs higher, and he pranced forward, one slow crunch at a time. No other hoofprints marred the sparkling surface of the pastures. Knee-deep in the fluffy powder, he soldiered on.

We followed the fence line uphill toward a wooded area, where I hoped the snow would be softer, less tiring for him than punching through the hard crust.

"Good boy, Caleb." I patted him on the neck.

Just inside the deep shade cast by the evergreen trees he stopped abruptly, his head up, ears at attention. He was peering at something in the woods. *A deer? A fox?* He turned his head left and right, adjusting his twin antennae to listen. After a few seconds' hesitation, I felt his back stiffen. Before I could reassure him, he wheeled on his hind legs and galloped straight down the steep hill toward the barn. I yanked with all my strength on the reins and shrieked, "Whoa, whoa. Stop! Ohhh no!"

If he headed to the upper door, we would be fine, but Caleb ran right past it. About halfway down, the slope steepened. I felt his back legs tuck under his hips as he started to slide. Twin arcs of snow flew up around his chest. Out of the corner of my eye, I caught a glimpse of Lou and Farley framed inside the middle doorway, their arms folded, faces blank. I screeched, "Helllllllp! I can't stop him!" even though

I was dimly aware that a person, or even two, couldn't stop a runaway animal. Clearly, I was on my own.

At that moment, Caleb veered away from the barn and careened down the hill, aiming straight for the ice-covered parking lot. Disaster lay thirty yards away. A horrific image flashed through my mind: Caleb and I sprawled on the ice, eight broken limbs and two broken necks jutting in random directions; the vet putting Caleb down while I waited to be hauled off to the hospital in the Bridgmans' old truck. Then again, up here in wild Wyoming County, the vet might put us both out of our misery.

At the bottom of the slope, Caleb locked all four legs and slid onto the ice. He spun and hopped as if attempting a double axel, me clinging to his neck, his short mane tickling my nose. We continued to slide sideways into the middle of the parking lot.

My breathing gradually changed from sobbing gasps to shorter gulps. "Okay, Caleb, we're still up. Don't move." My teeth clacked like castanets. I slid from the saddle, but when I struggled to stand, my boots slid beneath his icy belly, and I fell hard on my shoulder. He lowered his frost-coated muzzle between his front legs and stared at me. His breaths came out in rapid puffs of steam. Beneath his shaggy coat, he was shuddering. Oddly, his anxiety calmed me. For the first time, my donkey needed to trust me. I cleared my throat and said in a fairly calm voice, "Take it easy, Caleb. Don't move."

Afraid that he might fold up in a heap on top of me, I had no time to waste. I rolled onto my hands and knees. I could crawl toward the barn. But Caleb? What would he do? There was no way I would leave him out here alone, not even for a minute. Using Caleb's front leg for support, hand over hand I inched up to stand. One sudden move and we would both crash to the ground. Gently stroking his neck, I whispered into his ear, "Good boy. Easy now."

Either we collected ourselves, I reasoned, or we would be stuck here until the snow piled up and froze us into statues. It was clear that the Bridgmans wouldn't do a damned thing. Some hay or sand, some saddle blankets, or even a pile of manure thrown onto the ice would give us the traction we needed to reach the barn. As I stood rubbing Caleb's sweaty neck, I summoned a little fury at Farley's and Lou's lack of concern, which warmed me up nicely.

As if in answer to my prayers, the small door nearest to our position opened. Little Crystal in her pink cowboy hat stepped onto the ice, thought better of it, retreated to the doorway, and returned with a bunch of carrots. At this touching scene, terror shot through my chest. "Noooo, no, no. Don't!"

Too late. Caleb lunged toward the treats. His head far forward of his center of gravity, he skated stiff-legged straight to the door. Nearly there, his forelegs suddenly slid out from under him and his chin scraped the ice. He wrenched me off my feet, and I smacked my knees on the ice. He regained his footing and shuffled slowly to the barn door. I rolled onto my side and waited for the pain to subside before creeping crabwise toward the barn.

Inside, Caleb was nowhere to be seen. I limped down the long dark aisle to his stall. Someone had removed his saddle and bridle and had put him and his tack away. His ordeal over and apparently already forgotten, he snorted softly as he plucked a mouthful of fresh hay from the trough. Just then, my body was racked with a violent tremor that radiated from my knees to my neck, a delayed reaction to our near rendezvous with tragedy. To keep from crumbling into a heap, I hooked both arms over the stall door until my breathing slowly calmed. Unlike me, Caleb lived in the present. The barrage of what-ifs and horrific scenarios that flooded my brain more or less continuously had no place in his life. I watched him for a few minutes, before whispering, "Hey, Caleb. How's my boy? Pretty scary day, huh?"

Caleb lifted his head from the trough and ambled over to the stall gate. He placed his heavy head on my shoulder and rubbed his ear against mine. I stroked his velvety nose up and down until my breathing matched the rhythm. "We did it, didn't we? We trusted each other. See you tomorrow, big fella."

CHAPTER 6

Homecoming

ON NEW YEAR'S EVE MORNING I peered out my motel room's small window through a thick curtain of falling snow. It was a scene reminiscent of a Bergman film. Winter had settled in with a vengeance. Eighteen days of lessons, admonishments, and (mostly) unintended humiliation at the hands of the trainers, brightened by moments of their bizarre hospitality, were over. The progress I had made with Caleb, though fitful at best, provided at least some inkling of the challenges we would face in the months ahead.

Today, assuming that Laura Butti, the owner of Silver Rock Farm, could maneuver the stable's horse trailer over the local snow-covered roads, my donkey would be traveling to his new home near New York City.

Six months before I found Caleb, I had searched for a stable that would accept a donkey. It proved much harder than I expected. Throughout the spring of 2001, I had visited six stables near my home in Rockland County. When I asked the stable owners if I could board a donkey on their premises, they shook their heads. "Donkeys kick and bite. They're untrainable. Farriers and vets won't touch them."

Everything I had read about these animals suggested just the opposite, so I handed out copies of articles to prove that the myths about intractable donkeys were untrue. In the face of my relentless enthusiasm, the stable owners all fell back on their main weapon: they had long waiting lists for stalls. The owner of the fanciest stable implied that parents reserved stalls as soon as their future dressage champion was confirmed in utero. Stable after stable in the Hudson valley sent me away with the refrain: "A donkey? Why a donkey?" At the time, it was a reasonable question, one I hadn't been able to answer — even for myself.

Silver Rock was my last option, and I was grateful when Laura admitted that she was "intrigued" by my desire to have a donkey. Her precondition was that I would take riding lessons for six months before I bought one. She ran a large program for children with special needs, and she and her oldest pony, Patches, proved patient with this nervous adult rider.

From the start of our friendship, I shared every detail of my quest to find a donkey, and Laura seemed as excited as I was about bringing Caleb home. Though Silver Rock was a dressage stable, like all the others in the area — and dressage was the *last* thing I wanted to learn — I was heartened when she allowed me to ride Patches on a woodland trail next to the property. The narrow, interconnected pathways would suffice until I learned to control my donkey. A glance at the near-whiteout conditions outside the motel window dimmed the happy vision for the moment.

Late that morning, a truck towing a two-horse trailer slid to a stop in the unplowed motel parking lot. I ran outside to greet the Silver Rock employees. "Welcome to Siberia!" I yelled, almost in tears at the sight of familiar smiling faces. Bonnie O'Hara, one of Silver Rock's riding instructors, climbed down from the cab and landed in the knee-deep snow. I was glad she had come along. Despite her elfin size, she handled the biggest horses at Silver Rock with ease and good humor. With my rambunctious donkey, I desperately needed all the friendly help I could get.

On our way to the farm with my car in the lead, we caught up with the snowplow as it pushed the latest snow accumulation to the side. Here and there, twelve-foot-high banks of compacted snow threatened to topple onto the thin strip of pavement. I looked back at the truck and trailer fishtailing on the road down into Warsaw and back up onto the plateau. The driving conditions were iffy at best. A few miles beyond, I turned into the Bridgmans' driveway and coasted across the all-too-familiar icy surface. Safely parked, I trudged back to the road to guide the trailer in.

Just a few feet into the driveway, Laura's truck slipped sideways as it attempted the slight rise and plowed into a snowbank. Wrenching the truck from side to side, she reversed the cumbersome rig back onto the road. On her second attempt to enter the driveway, the back wheels of the truck slipped sideways and thumped against the banked snow. Laura backed up again, but this time she continued backing down the hill onto the road before pulling the rig over to the side and stopping.

Lou poked her head out her kitchen door and waved, hollering, "Coffee's on."

Laura and Bonnie walked up the drive to meet Lou. All business, Laura said, "We don't have time for coffee. We have to stay ahead of this storm."

As far as I could see, we were already way behind the storm. At least a month behind. With the horse trailer skidding all over the road, and the storm worsening by the minute, I hoped for a reprieve. I turned to Laura. "What if we wait until it stops?"

Laura turned to Lou. "When *will* it stop?"

"Oh, 'bout the end of February," Lou said. No one except me laughed. She added, "Once it starts, it snows pretty much every day around here."

"I have to get back to the barn," Laura said. "I have a New Year's date." She strode back down the drive toward the trailer to help Bonnie lower the ramp. She waved. "Okay, let's load up."

Inside the barn, I found that Farley had already put on Caleb's new monogrammed halter and had attached its matching turquoise-and-purple rope. As soon as the donkey's nose poked out the barn door and caught the wind, he reeled back on his haunches.

"Come on, sweetie." I stepped outside. "We're going to your new home!" As I tugged gently on his halter, my feet slid out from under me. I more or less shimmied up his front leg to stand up.

The poor beast had ridden on a trailer only three times in his life, and each of these trips had been less than thirty miles. Silver Rock Farm was 325 miles away. Sensing the tension around him, he tucked his head and tail and dragged his hooves as if on his way to the glue factory.

Laura stepped carefully over to help. "Gee, he's a lot bigger than I expected. I hope he fits in his stall." She gripped his halter and spoke right into his big ear, "Come along, big man. Walk on." Bonnie and I shoved against Caleb's flanks while Laura pulled. An urgency in Laura's voice overrode her calm, take-charge demeanor, with the expected result. He applied his four-hoofed locking brakes. This time all three of us slid to our knees.

Laura stood up, brushed off her pants, and said, "That's it! No more nonsense, mister!"

Farley joined us, and with one person at each flank, we manhandled our stiff-legged prisoner as far as the trailer ramp. Just then a fierce wind gusted up the hill, knocking us off our feet again. Caleb looked up at the snow-covered ramp leading up to the dark maw of the open trailer and planted his hooves again. As relentless as the weather, and possibly more determined than a donkey, Laura said, "Just leave this to me. Stay back!"

I patted the donkey's already-snow-caked back. "Poor thing. It's okay, sweetie."

Laura snapped at me, "Get out of the way, Margie. You're not helping."

Bonnie climbed into the trailer with an extra-long lead line and wound it around the bar inside. On the first attempt to winch him in, his neck stretched out like a giraffe's, leaving his hooves still rooted to the spot. Unless Bonnie wrenched his head right off and sent it barreling into the trailer by itself, this donkey was going nowhere.

Just then, a small black car spun up the hill and stopped across the road from the trailer. A man stuck his head out the passenger-side window. "Need some help, ladies?"

When no one answered, two huge men wearing boots and barn coats squeezed out of the car. Without waiting for directions or an explanation, each man hoisted one of the trembling donkey hind legs until Caleb's haunches rested on their shoulders. Ducking his flailing hooves and with Bonnie tugging from the front, Laura and me pushing his shoulders, we managed to stuff a squirming, terrified donkey up the ramp and inside. Bonnie quickly clipped Caleb's halter to a short rope as Lou slotted the back bar in place. The guys picked up the ramp, already coated with an inch of new snow, and slammed it shut, sending a shudder and a snow shower right through the trailer. After I thanked them fervently, they returned to their car but waited.

I climbed into the front door near Caleb's trembling head to reassure him. "It's okay, Caleb." It felt anything but okay. He snuffled and gasped in between brays, snot and saliva freezing on his whiskers. My heart went out to him; he had no idea where we were headed or why. And I felt helpless to make the situation better. "This isn't good for him," I said. "Let me towel him off and put his new blanket on."

"He'll be fine," Laura said, with a touch of exasperation. I wanted to believe her. She was always the voice of calm and reason at her stable. She looked up at the sky and said, "We've got to go."

Just in time for our departure, the rate of snowfall had increased from heavy to blinding. Laura and Bonnie climbed into the cab. As the truck's wheels slithered sideways toward the ditch, Lou, Farley, the men, and I pushed the side of the truck and trailer until Laura guided the rig back up onto the crown of the road.

As soon as they made traction up the steep hill, I ran back to the house, hugged Lou, and ran for my snow-shrouded car. Lou called out, "Don't you want to fill a jerry can with water? He's used to it."

"No time, I'm afraid," I said as I reversed across the drive. I was already deferring to Laura, the horse expert in charge of my donkey's new home, over Lou's lifelong expertise with donkeys and mules. I hoped I wouldn't regret leaving the water behind.

"Call when you arrive, you hear?" Lou said.

"Thank you for everything, Lou." I turned toward the trailer. "I hope we make it."

"Me, too," she called, as she hurried toward the barn door.

Our vehicles slithered back onto the main road and headed toward Warsaw. On the downhill stretch into town, the truck slalomed right through the traffic light at the bottom of the slope. On the way out of town, I fell far back and watched with mounting dismay as the trailer tacked back and forth across both lanes, straining to clear the crest of the hill.

East of the county line, the clouds broke up, and the falling snow fell in soft veils. Even so, Laura's truck struggled up the last slope, slipping sideways from ditch to ditch before turning south onto the connecting highway. Once we turned onto the interstate, Laura raced off. Soon I couldn't keep up with her, even at eighty-plus miles an hour. I lost sight of the trailer for the last time soon after we turned east onto Route 17, a two-hundred-mile stretch of divided highway through the Catskills. My dread turned into outrage. Was this responsible driving? A couple of hours later, long after my last glimpse of the trailer, I began to fear I might not have Caleb very long, after all. Images of a bloody wreck, of twisted metal in a snowy ditch, flashed across my mind. If Laura kept driving so fast, she and Bonnie were headed for the Pearly Gates, with my donkey tooting his trumpet.

"Sheesh, Laura," I said, "can't your date wait?" I had seen her friend Bruce Mason at the barn. He'd started riding lessons about the same time I did. I had smiled to see another adult being led around on Patches.

I reached Silver Rock Farm in a state of postfury funk less than five hours after leaving Bridgman Stables. The trailer hadn't arrived. I paced around the barns, unable to contain my anxiety. Despite my upset mood, I still found myself impressed by the stable's size and level of activity. Even on New Year's Eve, both the outdoor rings were full of riding students, their instructors calling out commands. All four paddocks were filled with horses or ponies, each wearing its own fitted blanket.

Fifteen minutes later, the truck and trailer inched down the driveway. Sure that I would find four frozen donkey legs connected to a stiff corpse in the back, I was thrilled when a pair of long ears appeared behind the icy window. A hoarse, snuffling plea sounded from deep inside the trailer.

Laura and Bonnie emerged from the truck cab. Relieved that all had arrived in one piece but overwhelmed from hours of fear, I blasted Laura about speeding on the snowy roads. She said in a placid voice, "Did we? Once we reached the interstate, the roads were clear."

"You drove over three hundred miles in less than five hours! The roads were a mess!"

"Well, we made it okay, didn't we?"

I couldn't argue with that. Bonnie, Andre (the stable manager), and I joined Laura as she lowered the trailer ramp. The inside walls were coated with ice from Caleb's sweat and breath. He was shaking all over. Unloading him proved nearly as difficult as loading him. The poor donkey's joints seemed to have locked. Two of us needed to push on his chest and two more to pull his tail to back him down the ramp. I was shocked to see that he was coated with icicles of frozen sweat and rushed to fetch towels and his new blanket from my car.

Meanwhile, Laura, Bonnie, and Andre turned toward a commotion in the main ring. The horses in the ring bucked and reared and bolted to the far end with their terrified riders. An instructor sprinted past, shouting, "One of the horses in the barn leaped over his stall door! I can't believe it!"

"What's happening?" I asked Laura.

"The horses have never seen a donkey before." She seemed unconcerned.

"It's like we brought in a mountain lion!" Andre said.

Laura, serene despite the mayhem, and I guided a stiff-legged and dazed donkey around the barn to his new stall. Horses inside the barn kicked their stalls and snorted. One horse galloped past us and around the barn, with Andre and another girl in hot pursuit. Andre called over her shoulder, "He leaped right out of the paddock!"

If these expensive horses were freaking out and injuring

themselves or their riders, I was sure that Laura wouldn't let my donkey stay here, after all. I reminded myself that Silver Rock was the only stable in the county that would accept him. All of a sudden I feared that bringing him here had been a big mistake.

Laura disappeared into her tiny unheated office, re-emerging five minutes later in a silvery-green velvet jump-suit, a pearl necklace, and low suede boots. She said, "Have to be off. He'll be fine. Let him settle in." She tottered across the snowy drive, climbed back into the mud-and-salt-encrusted truck, and drove off for her date.

The barn was closing soon, but I wanted to fuss over Caleb a little. Unlike the other horses, an old mare named Ginger welcomed her odd-looking next-door neighbor. She stuck her head over the gate and nickered at him as I brushed his soggy fur. After I put on his new blanket and was closing the gate, I noticed a brand-new shiny brass nameplate affixed to it: CALEB's DREAM, OWNER MARGIE WINSLOW. Laura had told me a few weeks earlier that the donkey should sport a fancier name, given that Silver Rock Farm was, after all, a *dressage* stable. She'd added the "Dream" part.

"Poor Caleb. More like a nightmare for you, isn't it?"

He stuck his head over the stall gate, a mouthful of hay dangling from his lips. I passed him an apple and said, "Happy New Year, Caleb. You're home now."

Caleb's new home at Silver Rock Farm (photo by Margaret Winslow)

CHAPTER 7

Disaster

ONLY A WEEK AFTER CALEB'S ARRIVAL at Silver Rock, the phone rang and woke me up. I rolled over in the dark and squinted at the clock on my nightstand: 5:45 AM. I picked up the receiver. Before the phone reached my ear, Laura spoke softly. "Margie, it's Laura. Don't panic."

Nothing makes me panic faster than when someone tells me not to panic. I croaked out, "What's wrong?"

"Don't be upset. It will be okay," she said in the same neutral voice, before adding, "but get your butt over here as soon as possible."

I had never heard Laura speak this way before. Certainly not to me. Did her tone imply I had been grossly negligent in some way? Or was she camouflaging her own fears by talking tough? I sat on the edge of my bed, my toes searching for my slippers. "What is it? Is it about Caleb?"

"He's colicked. Maybe a twisted gut. He's soaked in sweat and breathing hard."

"Oh no!" I cried. I knew that it was essential to keep a horse with colic on his feet and moving, or else it could be fatal. Twisted gut was far worse. Some breeds of horses and dogs can develop twisted gut just by rolling over, which can cause the stomach to flop over itself and cut off circulation. Were donkeys susceptible? "Is he up?" I asked.

"Yes, yes, I got him up. Come as soon as you can."

"Can I bring anything?"

"Some towels? Carrots? Never mind; just get here."

I raced to throw on long underwear and sweats. I guzzled milk from the carton and grabbed a bag of carrots and some towels. Halfway to the car, I turned and ran back inside to scoop up three recently purchased reference books on donkey health. A moment of clarity.

On the six-mile drive to the stable, I tried to clear my head. Only yesterday, Andre had observed to me, in what seemed an offhand way, "He hasn't eaten or drunk much water in more than twenty-four hours." Her flat comment didn't arouse panic, because, quite frankly, his docile, even laid-back, behavior since arriving at Silver Rock had seemed like a blessing, compared with the rambunctious beast I had struggled with at the Bridgmans' training school. Why hadn't I sensed something was wrong with my donkey?

I pounded the steering wheel, waiting for the light to change, forcing myself to exhale. Maybe colic wasn't so bad. That was what babies got all the time, wasn't it? Then I remembered Laura's beloved horse Bruno and whispered,

"Oh my God." Last spring when I had just begun lessons at Silver Rock, Bruno developed twisted gut and had to be euthanized less than two hours after the onset of his symptoms. His agonized thrashing and groans were unbearable to witness.

Of all people, Laura would know what Caleb's rapidly worsening symptoms meant. All prey animals are stoics. In order to avoid being singled out by wolves or lions, they will avoid limping or gasping or crying out until they fall down near death. An openly suffering animal, therefore, is extremely ill. At least an hour had passed since Laura found my donkey soaked in sweat and panting. How long had he been suffering before she found him?

With Bruno in mind, I steeled myself for what I might discover when I reached the farm. As soon as I parked, I ran over to Laura, who confirmed the worst. "He's colicked, for sure," she said. "Hope it's not twisted gut." She filled me in on the details. When she had arrived, she came across a stricken Caleb, lying down and groaning in his open stall. She had wrenched him to his feet and called the vet, then me.

Besides not eating or drinking or producing manure, the clearest signs that Caleb had colic were that he had bitten and kicked his flank. "The vet will be here in forty-five minutes," she said. That seemed an awfully long time to wait for medical treatment, but the nearest large-animal vet served several counties in the lower Hudson valley.

I trotted around the outside of the barn and looked into the shadowy stall, dreading what I might see. In the darkest corner of his stall, Caleb stood facing the back wall, his head down and his ears hanging limp. Sweat had soaked his coat and ran in rivulets down his side.

"Caleb, my buddy. What's wrong? Feeling bad?"

Ginger nickered and tossed her head, agitated. I stepped inside and toweled his sopping-wet back, while a sharp January wind blew past the open top half of the door. Up close I could see that his ribs were heaving. Small steaming "huffs" came out his throat as he exhaled. I rubbed harder. Laura joined me and helped towel him off before putting on his halter.

"What else can I do?" I asked Laura.

"Keep him on his feet and moving." She stepped out of the stall and said over her shoulder, "Whatever you do, don't let him lie down!"

I attached the rope and pulled. He wouldn't budge an inch. Laura called back to me. "You've got to get him moving!"

I tugged again, harder, whispering to him, "Take a step. Please, Caleb, just one."

Laura disappeared around the corner, returning with a six-foot-long whip. She whapped him sharply on the rump. He plodded a step or two and stopped, his sides heaving from the effort. She handed me the whip and strode off. There was no way that I could apply it to my suffering donkey, so I tossed it outside the stall. Repeated begging and tugs on his halter, though, induced him to take just one more step.

A few minutes later, Laura entered the stall with a huge syringe with a six-inch needle. I jumped aside, staring.

"I'll give him some bute," she said. "What's the dose for a donkey?"

"Oh no. I don't know. Donkeys are different from horses. I think they require less medication for their size." Or was it more? I dimly recalled reading that donkeys metabolized drugs at a different rate than horses. But was it faster or slower?

Laura didn't wait on my dithering. She plunged the six-inch-long needle into Caleb's shoulder and injected the phenylbutazone, a potent painkiller. He hardly flinched. Soon his breathing slowed, but all our cajoling and tapping with the whip couldn't get him to move more than an inch at a time.

"Where the hell is the vet?" I asked her. As if on cue, a truck rumbled down the drive and parked behind the barn. Dr. Maria Laurendeau, whom I had met when she had tended Bruno, stepped down from the truck. Tall, slim, with shoulder-length gray hair gathered into a single braid, she looked like a young Western rider. The jeans, work boots, and canvas coat completed the picture.

"So this is Caleb," she said, leaning on the stable door. "Looks a bit low."

Just then her cell phone rang. As she turned away, she said to me, "I was on my way to the raceway." She spoke into the phone, "Yeah. I'll be there. Got a colicky donkey. Yeah, that's right. A *donkey*. Be over later." So, the million-dollar racehorses could wait. My trust in Dr. Maria soared. She stepped into his stall and commenced her exam. "Hmm. Look at his gums. They're pale, at least compared to a healthy horse. Are they usually this pale?"

I shrugged; I hadn't noticed. The vet pinched the skin on his neck. "His skin should bounce back right away. See how it is? He's severely dehydrated."

"It's all my fault," I said in a wavering voice. "I should have exercised him more. And I gave him some dried apple slices. Maybe he wouldn't drink the unfamiliar water."

Dr. Maria ignored the self-blame and slathered petroleum jelly on a foot-long thermometer, which she slipped under his tail. Caleb grunted at the intrusion. "What's the normal temp for a donkey?" she asked.

"Wait, I'll check." I tore off toward my car.

Seconds later I returned and nervously pawed through the indexes of the books, my vision blurred by tears. I was glad Caleb's new vet didn't assume that horses and donkeys were identical. By the time I located the right page, the vet had removed the thermometer and peered at the mercury level.

"Here it is," I said. "Their normal temp is a couple of degrees lower than a horse's."

"Hmm. So he has a real fever." Dr. Maria placed a red plastic stethoscope under his left armpit. "What's a donkey's normal heart rate?"

"Wait." My sweaty fingers flipped through the pages. "Okay. It says forty beats per minute."

"So his heart rate's up, too. And respiration rate's up."

Now I knew for certain that my donkey was in great distress. Next, she palpated his abdomen. "Hard as a rock." She bent down to place the stethoscope near his heart and all along the length of his belly. She straightened up, passing the stethoscope to me, and said, "Here, listen."

I twisted the earpieces to block the wind. "I can't hear a thing."

"Normally," Dr. Maria explained, "you hear constant rumbles and squeaks. Normal gut sounds."

I strained again to hear something — anything — that indicated he was normal. "Nothing."

"Exactly. Not good." Dr. Maria wrote something in a notebook. "When I return this afternoon, we'll see what we need to do."

"Wait. You're leaving?" I called to her retreating back. "What do you mean by 'what we need to do'?" I asked, my hands lightly stroking Caleb's neck.

"See if we can move the blockage."

The next several hours crept by as I cajoled the suffering donkey to drink some water, to walk, to do anything other than stare with glassy eyes at the back wall, panting. I patted Ginger and gave her the carrots Caleb wouldn't touch. She seemed as anxious as I was. Somehow it didn't occur to me to call the Bridgmans, perhaps because they were too far away to help. Or maybe because I feared their censure if I told them that, after just one week in his new home, my donkey was dying. "He was healthy when he left," they were bound to say.

With the winter sun slipping behind the wooded hills, I heard the roar of Dr. Maria's truck coming down the driveway. I dashed over to meet her. "He's the same, just the same."

She nodded and removed her bag from the back. "Let's see — he had his last shot this morning. How much bute can he take?"

"Not sure."

"His weight?"

"Maybe 650, maybe 700 pounds." So much I didn't know!

"Okay, let's get this done."

Dr. Maria slipped around the outside of the barn and returned with a foot-long syringe. Rigid with terror, I feared she might give him an overdose. I pawed frantically through the pages of my reference books but couldn't find any guidelines regarding dosage. Before I could express my concern, Dr. Maria plunged the needle into Caleb's neck. He jerked his head up a little and rolled his eyes, the first reaction I had seen all day.

"His breathing has slowed. He hasn't tried to lie down, has he?"

I shook my head. Dr. Maria motioned for me to follow her to her truck. In the back, she extracted two new five-gallon plastic buckets, yards of clear plastic hose, and two large funnels, which she handed to me. She then lifted out a gallon of bleach and two gallons of mineral oil and carried them to his stall. She laid the equipment in a pile, stepped into the stall, and inserted the thermometer under his drooping tail. "His temp's down a little. That's good," she said. "How's the donkey's airway and throat constructed? Seems I remember it is different from a horse's."

"Yes. There's something about that in one of my books."

Here's where my academic research and insatiable curiosity about all things donkey-related paid off. I scrambled to find the article and set of diagrams I vaguely remembered on donkey anatomy. Something about a pouch or bend that makes insertion of a feeding tube difficult.

"Here it is." I showed her the diagram. Dr. Maria glanced at the page and nodded. She sterilized the buckets and funnel right outside Caleb's stall, pouring a gallon-size jug of bleach into the buckets, swishing it around, and dumping it on the ground.

"Here. Fill one of the buckets half-full of water and rinse them out."

Caleb stared dully over the half door at the goings-on, his first show of interest in the world since his ordeal had begun. Thanks to the painkiller, he hardly fussed when

Dr. Maria fed the tube up into his velvety nostril and down his throat. With funnel attached and held high, she poured mineral oil straight from the jug, quarts and quarts of it coursing through the tubing and right into his stomach. He shook his head and tried to back away, but Laura and I hugged his trembling neck until the mineral-oil jug was empty. Dr. Maria gently withdrew the hose, dumped it into the bucket, added some bleach, and washed it. Next, she lifted Caleb's tail, inserted a length of well-greased hose, and proceeded to pour another gallon of mineral oil into the funnel.

Caleb's eyes bulged and rolled, and he shifted his weight from one hoof to the next. I buried my face in his neck fur to block out the image.

When she had finished, I asked her about Caleb's chances of recovery. "Possible, if it's just a small blockage. Not so good, if it's a twisted gut." She caught my terrified expression and added, "There's still time. We just have to wait and see."

After Dr. Maria drove away, I waited anxiously for a result — an explosion, perhaps? Surely all that added liquid would worsen his pain. Caleb stood, facing the door, his head lowered.

My job was to report to Laura if he attempted to lie down or if he collapsed. Grazing animals, I had learned during my crash course on colic, need to move their legs to keep their digestion flowing. But even my desperate pleas to "walk on" couldn't budge him from his stall. I stopped pushing on his rump and decided to rub his hard belly and brush his thick winter coat instead. I sang a jaunty Gene Autry song, mostly to cheer myself up. "Back in the saddle again…"

He continued to face the back wall of his stall, his dark eyes turning toward me only when I cajoled him with baby talk: "Turn around, honker-donker. Please look at me!" It took all the courage I had to keep smiling through my tears.

The next morning I arrived at the stable in bright sunshine. Before I reached Caleb's stall, I asked the stable manager the Big Question. "Has he, you know, gone to the bathroom yet?"

"And how," Andre said, a disgusted look on her face.

"Wonderful!" I said.

Andre looked like she wanted to kill someone. "Had to move him to another stall until we clean up the mess."

Mount Saint Caleb had erupted! I was giddy with relief. I dashed toward his temporary residence, where a big white head jutted over the top of the stall door. "Good boy! That's my honkey-donk!"

He nodded, eyes half-closed, and belched in my face. I sank my face into his neck fur and wept in relief. That night I slept deeply for the first time since Caleb had arrived at Silver Rock.

CHAPTER 8

The Donkey Ambassador

DURING CALEB'S CONVALESCENCE, winter returned, and the ground was soon covered by a thin layer of snow. Every day I walked him around the barns and down the driveway. *Step, stop, step, stop.* Our labored progress forced me to slow down my constantly racing thoughts. During those hours, all I desired was Caleb's warmth and the sound of his clopping hooves at my side. For the first time in many years, I felt almost serene. A solitary child, I had often fled the strife between my parents by going on long walks. When I was an adult, long field seasons alone in the wilderness had calmed me from conflicts at work or in relationships. Joe and I found reflections of each other in that same way. Lucky for him, he was still traveling as part of his job; I was mostly stuck at home.

In his oversize winter blanket, Caleb looked small and vulnerable. When I draped my arm over his neck and his warm fur tucked right under my armpit, he felt exactly like Francis, my toy donkey, did when I was a child. He responded by rubbing his nose up and down the front of my jacket and resting his heavy head on my shoulder.

Caleb slowly regained his strength, and with it his outgoing personality returned. Far from his quiet home in rural upstate New York among sheep and goats, he now found himself the center of attention. Dozens of people passed his stall every day. Kids, especially, stopped to touch his impossibly long ears or to offer a treat. Even the sometimes withdrawn or fearful kids in the handicapped program were instantly charmed by the comical-looking beast.

For all I had read about the donkey's solitary nature, as soon as I put his halter and lead rope on, he dragged me all over the grounds to greet people. It was as if Caleb had set himself up as the ambassador of donkeys. He nodded as he majestically accepted tributes from his new fans. He often followed up, though, by snatching zipper pulls, mittens, and ski caps. After the uproar among the horses Caleb had caused when he first arrived, I was pleased to see that he could charm the bill-paying customers.

While extricating stolen treasures from Caleb's eager grip, parents often asked, "What kind of donkey is he?" They were referring, of course, to his unusual height and color. In this upscale New York suburb crammed with McMansions, people were unsatisfied with "He's just an oversize donkey." Not that I was status-conscious. *Not me.* If I had been, I would never have bought an animal so many people thought of as slow and stupid.

I had to admit, though, that sometimes I felt a bit defensive about my unusual choice of companion animal. Teenage girls seemed to zero in on my insecurity. One stopped by Caleb's stall and, after a few polite general questions about differences between donkeys and horses, got right to the point: "Why didn't you buy a *real* horse?"

I couldn't resist a wisecrack answer: "He was advertised as a Thoroughbred on eBay." When that failed to raise a smile, I amended it to: "Maybe I typed in 'eBray' by mistake." That worked.

I thought he was pretty special, of course, so I studied every reference book I could find. After all, I am a teacher. I found the terminology a bit confusing, as several definitions overlapped. The obvious way to classify donkeys is based on their shoulder height. There are very few breed registries for donkeys in the United States, in contrast to many such groups for horses (Morgans, Clydesdales, Paso Finos, and so forth). Those categories that do exist are for the two height extremes: miniature donkeys and mammoth jackstock. Miniature donkeys must be less than thirty-six inches tall. Mammoth jackstock require a minimum height for jacks (males) of fifty-six inches and fifty-four for jennets (females). Mammoths are the premier choice for creating big draft mules from draft mares, such as those once used by the US Army and still used by the Amish and some other traditional farmers. All donkeys whose heights fall in between miniature and mammoth come under the bland category of "standard," which is subdivided into small, medium, and large. At fifty-four inches, Caleb lacks two inches in height to qualify as a mammoth donkey, and thus is categorized as a large standard.

Since people often asked, I tried to unravel the confusion regarding the term *burro*. In Spain, a *burro* is a small donkey; *asno* refers to a large one. In the United States, *burro* is used for the feral donkeys that roam across the West, a term analogous to *mustang*, which refers to feral horses. The burros were brought to the Americas by Spaniards in the 1500s. Caleb certainly doesn't fit the characteristics of a burro, with its stocky, short midsection, potbelly, and up-curved nose. They are usually fawn gray or dark brown with white muzzles and bellies. When "conformation," or other physical characteristics besides shoulder height, is considered, however, the definitions blur a bit. Although Caleb is a little short of the mammoth measure, his long muzzle and ears and long, wide back fit in with the mammoth criteria. Going a little deeper, there are two lineages of large Spanish donkeys that created the mammoth breed in America. One is all white; the other dark brown with a tan muzzle and underbelly. In Europe they retain their original names: Andalusian and Catalan (or Catalonian), respectively.

Since people insisted Caleb was not like any other donkey they had ever seen, I began to call him an "Andalusiantype saddle donkey." What I thought was a somewhat fanciful definition was actually confirmed when, on a business trip to Spain, I showed pictures of Caleb to several donkey experts. They declared, *"No es un burro; ¡es un asno real!"* ("That's not a burro; he's a royal ass!") — meaning one of the large white saddle donkeys bred for the aristocracy of yesteryear.

That Caleb might be a royal ass in another sense soon became abundantly clear.

CHAPTER 9

Lead Line

CALEB'S FIRST SPRING at Silver Rock arrived with bursts of flowers. One afternoon, I fled my office early so that I could hand-walk Caleb. I hoped that a pleasant walk would offset the helpless rage I felt at my college administration's latest scheme. Just that morning the provost had demanded that we determine the value of teaching spaces by the revenue generated per student (tuition, presumably) per square foot! The concept was so ridiculous that emails flew back and forth inquiring whether heavyset students and lecturers counted more than slim ones.

I loved to groom and exercise Caleb whenever I could. Animal behaviorists might call it "imprinting," which to me sounded like inserting a microchip into him or maybe some form of cyber-brainwashing. I call it love and affection. I especially wanted to reinforce the bond we had formed during his illness. And I was getting worried. Gone was the meek, convalescing donkey I had escorted around the barns. Caleb's mischievous side had reemerged with a vengeance. When I threw my arms around his neck, he nipped me. When I joined him in his stall to groom him, he sometimes slammed me into a wall or kneecapped me. My howls of pain and weak-armed shoves were met with flashing eyes and increased high jinks. Lou Bridgman had warned me to conceal any signs of pain or fear, as that would show him his own strength, but sometimes it was impossible. It was paramount that I stay ahead of my smart but rebellious student, at the very least for the safety of others at the stable.

I parked and rushed directly to his stall. His head rested on the stall door, eyes closed, as he dozed in the last rays of the afternoon sun. "Hi, Caleb. Let's go for a walk?"

He tilted his head and gazed at me through long white eyelashes, yawning, as if to say, "Oh, it's you again."

I opened the stall door and stepped inside, where the warm odors of hay and donkey relaxed me somewhat. And that's when everything changed. Caleb spun his hip around and mashed me against the wall.

Though friendly and curious by nature, donkeys, unlike horses, are territorial and especially hate to feel cornered. I recalled Lou's warning that I should enter a donkey's stall only briefly, to put on his halter, attach the lead line, and lead him out. "This is *his* space," she said. Caleb had already slammed a muscular farm employee into the wall when he had entered, pitchfork blades flashing. From then on, his stall was cleaned only when Caleb was outside.

"Okay, okay. I'm thrilled to see you, too! Ouch! No nipping! Come on, boy, I don't have much time today." He tossed his head to evade the halter and grabbed the rope in his mouth before I could attach it.

Finally, I got his halter and lead rope in place and guided him from his stall. I eyed him. He tilted his head toward me and batted his eyelashes seductively. *He's sizing me up.* I aimed for an alpha Laura tone: "Don't even think about it, buster." Caleb dropped his head and trudged forward.

Just as we turned the corner of the barn and entered the busy driveway, he lunged, dragging me with him. "Whoa! Stop, damn it!" I gripped the rope with both hands, leaned back, and planted my feet. My armpits stretched, and the gritty rope flayed my bare hands as it slipped through my palms. When the last inch of rope ripped away, Caleb bolted right into the path of a continuous parade of shiny SUVs and vans that were nosing into parking spots next to the ring. I caught up with him when he stepped on his trailing rope and stood, blinking with surprise, wondering what had stopped him. Before he could move a hoof and magically release himself, I pounced on the rope.

With Caleb standing square in the middle of the drive-way, all traffic entering Silver Rock came to an abrupt stop. To make things worse, the hay truck, the farrier, and the vet decided to arrive at the same time. Now at least a dozen people had front-row seats to watch our tug-of-war.

I pulled on the line. "Come on, Caleb. Let's move out

of the way. Please?" This wasn't the first time he'd decided to drop anchor in that spot, but I still believed that if he understood the predicament we were in, he would make some effort to please me. I was wrong.

I held tight and stretched the rope in a vain attempt to reach a fence post. Meanwhile, Caleb leaned back in classic stubborn-donkey pose, his neck and head flat out, haunches and tail tucked under his belly, his center of gravity low over those powerful flanks. A distant echo of Lou Bridgman's chuckle rattled in my ear: "You'll never win a tug-of-war with a donkey." *No kidding.* But if I could loop the rope around something, I might ratchet Caleb in, or at least move him far enough to the side so that vehicles could pass.

As a last-ditch effort, I backed away several yards and barreled up behind him and tried to push him out of the way by shoving his skinny butt. I succeeded only in planting my face in his tail. Another of Lou's bits of wisdom popped into my head: "If you're in a hurry, a donkey will take all day." In other words, the more desperate and anxious I became, the more he bided his time.

Parents stood by their cars. Some snickered; others frowned. They glanced at their watches or cell phones, impatient to drop off their daughters and be on their way. Amazingly, no one honked or swore, revved their engine, or attempted to dodge the donkey and his hapless owner.

I was mortified. In my stained denim overalls and Joe's

cast-off flannel shirt — both hastily pulled on over my teaching clothes — and my muddy rubber boots, I looked like a gold prospector caught thousands of miles from home and a century too late. My choice of stable wear, which had blended in perfectly at the Bridgmans', looked ridiculous at Silver Rock.

It soon became clear: I couldn't detach myself from my wayward donkey, physically or emotionally. The umbilical cord of gritty rope that connected us was the most visible manifestation of our struggling relationship. If I let go, he'd run amok and raid the barns or the grain shed or — far worse — barge into the ring, disrupting a lesson, possibly panicking a horse and throwing its rider. That had already occurred once. If it weren't for the hair-trigger reflexes of Laura, who grabbed the tumbling rider, a little handicapped girl would have been thrown when the normally placid old Patches reared in terror.

Soon my arms would be too weak to haul Caleb back to his stall. Maybe that was his goal. But who knew what new fancy might pop into his bony head? I carefully switched hands on the rope to give my raw fingers a rest. The unspoken message from Laura and other horse owners was: *it's up to you to make him behave.* All too often, Andre, instead of lending a hand, would shout at me, "Can't you control him *at all?*"

As if to underscore my incompetence, small girls tripped past in their immaculate jodhpurs and high-heeled riding boots, leading horses twice Caleb's size on short, slack reins. The huge horses trailed behind their young riders like well-oiled pull toys.

I growled, "Damn it, Caleb. Please don't do this to me."

Unlike me, Caleb didn't seem to be stressed at all. He was oblivious to the people and tons of grumbling metal that extended all the way out to the highway. I hissed at him, "You're making me look like a fool!"

I hadn't surrendered, not yet. If Caleb outdistanced me in strength and vigor, we were a match when it came to tenacity. Besides, I suddenly realized, the solution lay almost within my grasp. There was an eighteen-inch curb chain (also called a lead shank) attached to one end of the rope. If the lead line represents gentle but firm guidance, wrapping the curb chain around the animal's muzzle is about sheer coercion. Brute force, pure and simple. The one time I had used it at Silver Rock, Laura had asked, "Must you use the chain?" No other horses at Silver Rock were "curbed" this way. Dreading her disapproval, I hadn't used it since. Yet, Lou Bridgman's words echoed through my head: "Always use the curb chain when hand-walking a donkey. It's the only emergency brake you have." It was also useful to get a stubborn donkey to move. Just what I needed at that moment.

There was only one problem: in order to wrap the chain extension over and under the donkey's nose, I had to release the rope's clip from the halter's chin ring, thread it through the cheek ring around his nose, and reattach it to the cheek ring on the opposite side. Caleb had already demonstrated that he could wrench his head away at the worst possible moment, twist my fingers in the half-threaded chain, and trot off leadless and heedless wherever he wished.

While he remained rooted to the spot, staring placidly at the grille of the hay truck, I made my move. I released the clip under his chin and somehow rethreaded the chain through the side D rings, over his nose, and into the other side ring, all without Caleb exploding in a sudden bid to escape.

With the curb chain wrapped tightly around his muzzle and chin, I increased pressure on the rope. Caleb's pink freckled nose and nostrils pinched closed, but he stood his ground. I leaned back on the rope. His whole face puckered. He worked his jaws from side to side and shook his head in protest but finally, finally stumbled forward, one stubborn hoof at a time. I moved him off to the side and heard engines revving and switching gears as the traffic jam cleared. I kept up the pressure on Caleb's nose as we inched toward the barn. Mothers frowned as I man-hauled him past, the very picture of an ASPCA poster child of an abused donkey. One distraught mother said, "Oh, the *poor* donkey." I stifled my retort.

As a reward for the tiniest microscopic hint of compliance, I let up a little on the pressure, but Caleb took advantage of the slack and broke away. He darted off between two paddocks in search of something to munch on.

I'd had enough. With my dignity as shredded as my palms, I caught up with him, rump-deep in the prickly bushes. I stepped on his rope, abruptly halting him mid-chomp. He must have sensed that I had reached the end of my own tether, for he dropped his head and waited for the next move, chewing thoughtfully.

With wet sand now irritating the open scrapes on my palms, I reeled in the line until Caleb's freckled nose pinched into a grotesque mass. He performed his stiff-legged, toe-scraping, peevish-toddler act until we reached the side of the barn. Once we were out of sight, though, he pranced back to his stall, his head high, as proud as a winner of the Kentucky Derby.

"Thanks a heap, buddy," I said as I shoved the stall door closed on his rump.

A week later, I made my next big discovery: the lead rope doesn't work in both directions. That is, you can pull on it but not push. On the heels of the spring thaw, a ten-foot-wide, twenty-foot-long mini-lake of melt water blocked the driveway between the barn and the big ring. Other, smaller puddles dotted the property after every rainstorm.

I led Caleb right up to the giant puddle, intending to cross it as if it weren't there. I kept his focus on me using a short lead and talking into his ear. Just before his dainty hoof touched the water, though, Caleb jerked backward.

"Is it because you can't see the bottom?" Donkeys are wary of the unknown, so they will stop and contemplate for what seems like forever before taking a step. No plunging headlong into a bottomless quagmire despite its placid surface.

"I'll just have to show you, then." I stepped ahead, playing out the line, saying soothing things like "See, it's only a few inches deep." Near the center of the puddle, I stumbled into a hole; icy water flooded my boot. I suppressed a grimace. "Walk on, Caleb."

He wasn't having any of it.

I gradually increased the tension on the rope until his head and neck cantilevered over the murky water. Soon he would have to step forward just to regain his balance or else tilt headfirst into the muck. His ears pinned flat, nostrils dilated, he huffed noisily and snorted in fear.

Before I could plan my next move, the rope suddenly went slack. A rope will hold or pull an animal, more or less, at a fixed distance from the human but does nothing whatsoever when he suddenly *decreases* the distance. Caleb plowed straight into me. I lost my footing completely and sat down in the muck. Meanwhile, he reached the far side of the puddle and stood, watching me.

"Thanks a lot, bud." I sloshed over to a dry spot and stood up. End of lesson. After all, he'd done what I'd asked. We squelched back to the barn: an immaculately clean donkey, except for his hooves, and me, smeared with mud up to the hips and elbows. Andre turned away and coughed before I saw the look on her face.

As I drove home for a hot shower, I wondered whether, in the dimness of his stall at night, Caleb reviewed the day's events and chuckled to himself at my expense. I was almost convinced that the crafty rascal was keeping score.

CHAPTER 10

Back in the Saddle

PUSH, PULL. WAIT. BEG. TRY AGAIN. Later that spring, we set a new record: only fifteen minutes to wrestle Caleb a hundred yards from his stall to the big ring. It was time to ride him on my own. Up to this point, other than our nearly disastrous ride in the snow and ice at the Bridgmans', I had ridden him only during lessons at their stable. I hadn't ridden him at all at Silver Rock. Instead, day after day, I had hand-walked him all over the property, through the plant nursery, and on the trails next to the reservoir. I finally had to admit to myself that, frankly, I was putting it off. Although I was more than a little nervous, I looked forward to riding Caleb without the critical eyes of trainers focusing on our every misstep.

Inside the ring, I surveyed the layout. The sand-filled 180- by 60-foot rectangle enclosed numerous assorted jumps and barrels, with a large open space around its perimeter. Thankfully, no one else was using it.

There was no portable mounting block, so I needed to line Caleb up next to a long log-and-earthen bench adjacent to the outer rail. I walked him up to the bench and put one foot in the stirrup. But when I did, he walked off. After several repetitions of this slapstick show, I borrowed my next inspiration from Western movies. I attempted a flying mount. I ran up and hopped onto the bench, towing Caleb alongside. Then, like a bank robber fleeing Dodge City, I threw my torso across the saddle as he trotted by. Unfortunately, I overshot and landed headfirst on the other side. Sprawled on the ground, dusty but intact, I looked up at Caleb, who stood still, the picture of an obedient animal, his head lowered to stare at me through his legs.

"Now you're standing still. *Now?*"

Without a moment to spare, I tried again — the run up onto the bench, the leap. I threw myself across his back. This time I stayed on, although my legs dangled from one side, my arms and head from the other. As he wandered toward the center of the ring, I pivoted like a gymnast on a balance bar until I could swing one leg over and sit up.

I would have thought that all the energy Caleb showed during the fifteen minutes I had wasted mounting would continue afterward. But *no.* As soon as I was settled into the saddle, he stopped dead.

This led to my next challenge: finding the donkey's accelerator. Ages passed as I stared at the backs of his ears, my legs kicking until they ached, my arms limp from thrashing his flanks with my riding crop. I loosened the reins and waited. He sighed.

"Damn it, Caleb. Waiting for paint to dry would be quicker!"

Minutes dragged on, and I wondered: Was he asleep? Caleb lowered his head to nudge an imaginary fly off his foreleg and then traced with his nose its invisible path across the field. Clearly something was going on in that great hoary head.

"Damn it! Get a move on!" I commanded in my best imitation of Farley Bridgman's voice. Caleb ignored me. Fortunately, no one was watching us.

Right on cue, the click of the gate latch heralded the arrival of two young women and their horses. They walked over to the earthen bench, mounted, and guided their horses around the perimeter. All told, it must have taken them each less than a minute to do it.

While the girls trotted toward the far end of the ring, Caleb decided to stroll over to the nearest jump. There he stopped and sniffed the orange crossbar as if it was a big carrot. Out of the corner of my eye, I noticed that the girls were lining up to vault this very jump.

"Could you move him out of the way?" one of them called.

I jerked the reins and kicked and tapped Caleb's hip with the whip, working up a powerful sweat in the process. Caleb, unconcerned, progressed from sniffing to licking the bar. Before I could react, he grabbed the wooden bar in his teeth and dislodged it. He then stared at it, fascinated. As long as I was the center of unwanted attention, I fell back on an old defense mechanism: I might as well entertain them. I quipped, "Sorry. He's in 'power-saver mode.'"

The girls found another jump to practice on.

At that moment the gate opened to admit another horse and rider. Caleb sensed freedom and dove through the gate before the girl could close it.

Thus ended our first solo riding session.

The second time in the ring, we repeated the same steps with identical results: the donkey wouldn't stand still when I mounted but then stopped cold right afterward. I breathed deeply to release the tension between my shoulders and focused on the big picture. The sun was shining, the crisp air filled with the aromas of new grass and budding leaves. Best of all, I was freed from the stuffy science building where I taught, which resembled a parking garage but without the charm. In comparison, Silver Rock's grounds, as unadorned as they were, seemed like paradise. Caleb, too, should have been happy: he was free of his little stall, which was the size of my own office but with a better view.

All I wanted him to do was to walk forward a few steps, turn, walk back, and stop. How taxing could it be? He started forward at what I called his "dead man walking" gait. Slow. Then slower. After ten steps he stopped.

At Silver Rock, lessons ran every day, all day and often into the evening. Even when Caleb agreed to move, I couldn't help but notice how conspicuous we were — the big white donkey with his lurching rider weaving like a drunken sailor down the straightaway. Whenever a crowd hovered nearby, he seemed determined to create a spectacle.

Humility may be a virtue, but many years had passed since I had been not only so truly incompetent at a task but also so visible. Yet, as much as I hated to look like a fool, I had chosen the very animal that — almost by definition — would make me do just that.

"Come on, Caleb. Please move one hoof. Just one little hoof."

It didn't help matters that I had ignored the Bridgmans' advice about using a Western bridle. The apparatus generally includes a bit with a port (or bend), long shanks, and a short chain under the chin. With this system, when the rider draws in the reins, the bit rotates so that the port presses on the tongue or the palate. At the same time, the chain pinches the chin. English-style riders never use the Western setup; in fact, it's banned from English events at horse shows altogether because it provides additional, perhaps unfair, control over the animal.

My "kinder, gentler" philosophy had led me to choose an expensive Myler Comfort Snaffle bit. Myler's brochure advises that when encountering resistance, "go *softer*." Not harsher. This philosophy, though counterintuitive, appealed to my sense of fairness. According to *The Complete Book of Bits and Bitting*, though, "the shaped mullen mouthpiece," like the Myler model I had chosen, "is the mildest in its effect." In other words, my bit provided no leverage whatsoever. No steering, no brakes. Just to hoist his head up from the ground, I would have to develop arm and shoulder muscles to rival Arnold Schwarzenegger's.

An abrupt swerve brought me back to the task at hand. Caleb was heading toward the jump again. What was it about that particular jump that so intrigued him? I steered him to circle it clockwise. Instead, he turned left and trotted toward the mounting bench. I had to admit that the direction I had chosen was entirely arbitrary on my part, so why not let him wander around a bit?

Just as I had done with him on my first ride at Brenda's, I adopted "auto-training." As soon as Caleb stopped, I squeezed the reins and said, "Whoa. Good boy," and scratched his neck. Taut reins were intended to convey the notion of staying stopped, but Caleb seemed to think that I had forgotten to release the reins and that he should proceed. So I said, "Walk on, Caleb." When he veered left, I squeezed the left rein and said, "Good boy."

Building on this principle, we blundered around the ring. No matter what he did, I'd say, "Good boy, Caleb," in case anyone was watching. He followed my instructions to the letter…or rather, I followed his. Okay, this approach was all ass-backward. I suspected Caleb knew it, too.

To tell the truth, besides my buying into the "gentling" versus "breaking" philosophy, there was another reason why I was such a softy with him: I wanted him to like me. I suspected that he would hate me if I punished him, and then he'd misbehave even more. Behind it all, at a deeper level that I didn't admit even to myself, was the fact that I was afraid of him — his size, his power. He could really hurt me if he set his mind to it.

I obviously needed help. Thankfully, Laura, though she was mainly a dressage instructor, had agreed to work with me to train Caleb. We would start the following week.

CHAPTER 11

Lessons with Laura

BY THE TIME I HAD WRESTLED CALEB to the big ring for our first lesson, I was already breathless and irritable. The situation at the college continued to weigh on me — almost every month a classroom or teaching lab was confiscated and rented to outside projects and start-ups. Though our department had been spared, it was only a matter of time before the wrecking ball swung our way.

Caleb mirrored my foul mood: his ears were pinned back; his tail whipped against his flanks to ward off all comers. I'd had no time to change out of my work clothes, and my new white blouse already sported flecks of half-chewed hay, and the seat of my black dress pants bore the unmistakable imprint of a muddy hoof from what I preferred to believe was a playful tap. Not a promising start.

I struggled to unbolt the gate with one hand, holding Caleb with the other. He danced around me, undecided whether to enter the ring or tow me away from it. Inside, finally, he clamped his jaws on the top rail of the gate so I couldn't close it. I pleaded with him: "Please, Caleb. Be nice. We have to do this." My words made no impact, so I rapped his nose and shouted, "Let go!" That worked.

Next, I had to mount him. Based on my previous attempts to get in the saddle without help, I figured I had a 33 percent chance of succeeding on the first try. When Laura arrived, I was sitting straight in the saddle, my posture erect, my hands holding the reins evenly, appearing more or less like a competent rider. I hoped she wouldn't notice the wet sand stuck to my shoulder from an unsuccessful launch.

"Good afternoon, Margie and Caleb. Let's begin by tracing a circle."

He completed part of a circle at a funereal pace before veering across the center of the ring toward the same jump he always chose. This time, instead of playing with the crossbar, he leaned against the outer support frame until it wobbled and fell in a heap of boards and pegs. Alone with Caleb I would have let him satisfy his curiosity until boredom set in. But with Laura trotting up to us carrying a twelve-foot-long lunge whip and clearly meaning business, I tightened the reins and kicked. I shouted at him, "No!"

Without a word to me or Caleb, Laura clipped a thirty-foot-long rope (called a lunge line) to his bridle and marched us back to our starting point. "Okay, tell him to walk on," she said.

I kicked and called, "Walk on," but the donkey remained frozen to the spot, gazing dreamily into the distance. Laura tapped him on the flank lightly. He ignored it. Next, she ran up behind us, snapping the whip on the ground behind his heels. At this, Caleb plowed forward and traced a curved path, more amoeboid in outline than circular.

After a few minutes, despite attempts to chew on the rope and to grab the lunge whip from Laura, Caleb didn't seem to mind tracing circles and figure eights, although his tracks for the latter resembled malformed pretzels. Forced yet again to sink to beginners' level tethered to the line, at least we performed more or less as asked, twice in one direction, twice in the other, as Laura gradually increased the radius.

That day, with far more patience than I ever had, Laura began to break my reflexive habit of tapping his flank with my heels to signal him to walk on, at the same time tightening the reins to regain my balance when he lurched forward — thereby signaling a halt. No wonder the donkey ignored his wiggling, tilting, jerking, flailing, mumbling rider. Instead, he kept his ears turned toward Laura, often, if not always, heeding her calm voice of authority.

All the finer points of equitation — my posture, leg position, elbows — seemed like fussy details to me, but Laura saw them as integral parts of training. She constantly reminded me to adjust the reins, sit straight, and keep my heels down, while all I wished was for Caleb to carry me more or less from point A to point B without major detours or mishaps. Was that too much to expect from a donkey?

Mercifully, our first lesson ended after about twenty minutes, giving me another twenty minutes to dismount and to manhandle my donkey back to his stall.

All in all, it wasn't a bad beginning.

It was clear from the outset that Laura assumed that Caleb could be trained much like a horse. As she was the only stable owner who would accommodate us, I felt in no position to argue. Jack Bridgman's colorful anecdotes and my own experience with my donkey suggested otherwise, but Laura had trained hundreds of riders to handle horses and ponies with varying personalities, some as balky as Caleb. I also rationalized to myself that he was smart enough to accomplish such lofty goals, if we worked very hard. He was young. In time, he would come to enjoy our lessons, even if I was lukewarm about some of the details myself.

Or, at the very least, I would be able to steer him.

The next three riding lessons followed the same sequence: the wrestling match at his stall door, beginning with a spinning donkey dodging the grooming brush and his tack, followed by the obstacle race between the barn and the ring, the acrobatic mount, attempts to trace a circle unaided, all ending with Laura coming to the rescue armed with her lunge line and whip.

Despite Caleb's attempts to convince both of us other-wise, Laura never assumed that donkeys were impossible to train; she just hit *restart* and introduced a new pattern. This went on for weeks. If his intractable behavior contin-ued for much longer, however, I feared she would give up.

Caleb and Laura (photo by Suzanne Vosburg)

"Caleb knows when you're not paying attention," Laura reminded me more than once, echoing Lou Bridgman's ex-act words. She noticed that without a specific goal — in other words, when free of an immediate crisis — my mind wandered toward problems at work. She could tell by the faraway look in my eyes, the slackening of the reins, the failure to heed her commands. At these moments I was turning into my absentminded-professor father. We kids used to say, "Earth to Dad. Earth to Dad. Come in, please."

On the other hand, in my role as a field geologist I'd had no trouble focusing — even hyperfocusing — while navigating through dangerous jungles or Arctic seas in pursuit of evidence of ancient earthquakes. I thrived when immediately confronted with seemingly insurmountable challenges in remote regions. *Physical* challenges, that is, not those involving other sentient beings. Now I had a seven-hundred-pound intractable behemoth, physically challenging but yet possessing an independent personality I only half understood. For his sake and mine, I was going to have to try harder.

As our lessons continued, I began to notice that Caleb seemed at least as distractible as I was. No activity or object, no matter how far away, escaped his full attention: a person leaning on the fence, a car coming down the driveway, a fresh pile of manure on the track. An old pile of manure. The worst occurred when someone opened the gate, whereupon Caleb stampeded to escape.

Outside of our lessons, I sometimes stayed to watch Laura instruct others. With both beginners and advanced students, she varied her methods to suit different learning styles. She often had her students swap horses with other riders to solve a particular issue. When working with beginners, especially, she used positive reinforcement and praised her students frequently. Her results impressed me. Horses traced perfect thirty-meter circles and figure eights for an hour straight, cutting neat grooves into the sand.

But her attitude toward recalcitrant horses and ponies during those lessons was nearly the opposite. Laura, in the ring, was strict, her corrections made with crisp commands or a flick of her whip. She was brisk — to say the least. She couldn't afford to put up with misbehaving animals that might injure a rider. As she once confided to me, liability insurance ate up a significant portion of her revenue. More than once I had seen balky, bolting, or bad-tempered animals kicked out of the barn, some for transgressions far less serious than Caleb's kicking, nipping, and running amok. And this was how he behaved on a *good* day. I worried that, if I couldn't control Caleb better, we would soon find ourselves homeless.

On the drive home from a particularly fraught lesson, my mind switched automatically to theoretical speculation. What if the donkey's constantly varying antics functioned as a survival strategy in the wild? If a predator couldn't anticipate the big animal's next move, it would be hard to corner him. An image of Caleb's latest lapse sprang to mind. Maybe, as a last resort, might a donkey's tap-dancing hooves and ear calisthenics make the puma or wolf choke to death on its own laughter? I would have to look this up.

During our next predictably frustrating lesson, I said to Laura, "Caleb is bored doing the same exercise over and over." Hadn't she noticed that his attitude after he completed a pattern was "Been there, done that"? His short attention span, reflecting my own, swiftly morphed into mischief.

Laura replied, "You're just making excuses for his naughty behavior." Farley Bridgman's words.

Nevertheless, later in the week, after watching Caleb tracing amoeboid and pretzel patterns in the ring, she said, "Donkeys like to learn new things, don't they? They need a challenge, right?" She apparently had forgotten that I had brought this exact observation to her attention just days before.

"Great idea," I said.

She had already set up a line of eight or ten traffic cones. Up to this point, Caleb had merely knocked them over or chewed them. Marching next to his shoulder, Laura guided us through the cones in a grapevine pattern, before repeating the exercise standing off to the side. Next, she unclipped the line and said, "Now, you do it," cuing us the whole way. An unexpected bonus of a new challenge: I was forced to focus, pushing my work-related worries to the back of my mind.

Caleb managed to weave through three cones before knocking over the next two. He sniffed the following two cones, then picked them up and shook them before dropping them. When we reached the end of the row, he picked up the last cone and trotted over to the fence, where he bashed it up and down on the top rail before hurling it over the side. His twitching ears and sly, sidelong glances at Laura gave him away: *So much for that cone!*

She caught up with us and tugged the reins, hard. "Oh no, mister! None of that." He jerked his head away, his eyes wide with fear, astonished that he had done anything wrong. Laura clipped him back onto the tether.

A step back for us.

Right before our next lesson, Caleb unexpectedly dragged me straight from his stall to the big ring. I mounted in the usual haphazard manner, and he threaded his way between the cones, both up the line and back, veering aside at one point but knocking over only one. Too bad Laura wasn't there to see it. When she joined us, Caleb set off again through the obstacle course, snatching the traffic cones and dropping them here and there until he had arranged them to his satisfaction, as if auditioning for a job with the highway department. After she fetched the lunge line and whip, he traced the pattern more or less correctly, though the tracings of his hoofprints resembled a pile of over-cooked spaghetti.

Regardless of our performance, Laura always ended the lesson with some small sign of success, even if it meant just starting and stopping on command a couple of times. "Good donkey! Good man!" she would say, patting his neck.

CHAPTER 12

Is This Donkey Love?

BY SUMMER, most of the horses and ponies at Silver Rock had grown accustomed to Caleb's smell or appearance — or whatever it was that had freaked them out at first. In fact, Laura reported that placing "Donkey," as she called him, in a paddock with a new arrival calmed the horse down. Soon, newcomers were placed in stalls near his, on the other side of Ginger, the sweet old mare who had watched so patiently throughout Caleb's sickness and recovery. At least my odd choice of steed was starting to contribute in a positive way to life at Silver Rock.

Ginger stuck her head over the stall gate and nickered softly at her uncouth neighbor whenever I led him past her stall. Everyone said, "She's his girlfriend. They can't stay away from each other." But it looked to me as if she considered Caleb her gawky, late-life foal. For his part, he seemed indifferent to her, but maybe he was just playing hard to get.

Her love wasn't entirely unrequited. Caleb liked to play

with the gate latches on his stall and in the paddock. He spent minutes tonguing and biting the metal bolts, chains, and clips, all the while shaking his head. I often arrived to find the mechanism covered in warm slobber. It was only a matter of time before he succeeded in releasing himself. And one day Caleb released his stall latch, then walked out and released Ginger's. He proceeded to lead her on an un-tethered romp — possibly a once-in-a-lifetime adventure for the old mare — through the barns and around the rings, with several barn employees in pursuit. I was touched that Caleb had chosen to release Ginger and not another horse. This convinced me that he found her special.

Over time, my long-eared Houdini honed his skills, getting out even when one latch became two. Finally, the stable manager added a clip with a spring action, which did the trick. Soon after clips were added to paddock gates and other neighboring stalls, as Caleb showed that mere chains and bolts were no match for him.

Despite our daily struggles in the ring, Caleb continued to be openly affectionate toward everyone he met. Hoofed animals show closeness by leaning against each other; resting their necks on each other's backs; or head-butting, nibbling, or snuffling. In his pushy way, Caleb nudged my shoulder or hip, and I welcomed the weight of his heavy head on my shoulder. I admit that I craved the warmth of his fur on my face or neck. Sure, he sometimes intertwined a front hoof around my leg to trip me up or kicked me when I attempted to clean his hooves. At times his nips were too frequent, and my slaps and cries came too late to deter him. He always seemed surprised, though, when I reprimanded him. As I well knew, what constituted horseplay for equines, unfortunately, could knock a person down or cause bruises.

Soon I sported a huge inventory of bruises and welts on my left breast and my neck, bottom, and thighs from his "playful" kicks and nips. I had already gone to work with a two-inch-wide purple hickey on my neck. From the smirks on students' and colleagues' faces, my blithe assertion that "my donkey did it" convinced no one. In fact, so many bruises bloomed all over my body that — and I wince to recount this — my gynecologist, after a routine examination, pressed a brochure into my hands and patted my shoulder as I dressed. With my glasses back on, I looked at the title: "Reporting Domestic Violence."

"Oh no!" I laughed in an overly hearty voice. "These bruises are from my donkey!"

Her brief glance and nod said it all: "I'm here if you want to talk about it." The next visit I showed her photographs of Caleb, which mollified her somewhat. At least I hoped so.

Despite the pain my donkey's nips and kicks caused, I remained convinced that they weren't malicious. He seemed genuinely taken aback when I yelled or thumped him on the side. When I met his sparkling eyes as he dodged and trotted away, he seemed to be saying, "It's just a game, silly. What's the fuss? You can bite me back, if you want. Go ahead, pluck out some of *my* hair."

To my chagrin, Caleb did not treat all humans with such good-humored high jinks or clumsy affection. When Dr. Maria attempted to administer his semiannual vaccinations, Caleb head-butted her right off the concrete platform. Evidently, he hated her after the dual mineral-oil treatments she had administered that saved his life. I learned two things I had avoided acknowledging before: first, Caleb's head butts were not always affectionate or gentle — they could seriously injure even an experienced adult — and second, donkeys, like elephants, never forgive or forget.

Quite by accident, I discovered a useful training tool, sort of the reverse of unconditional love. One day I was so fed up with Caleb's antics that I threw down the halter and lead and stomped away. I leaned against the side of the barn out of sight, taking deep breaths until my anger subsided. I didn't want to slap or yell at a donkey that was, after all, just acting like a donkey.

No sooner had I turned the corner than Caleb began to snuffle. Soon his grizzling grew into a full-throated lament. When I returned, my eyes focused on the ground, he abruptly stopped braying and sighed. His head drooped, and he stood like a poor misunderstood beast, waiting. I came up and finished grooming and tacking the chastened donkey silently — no cuddles or treats this time. Until that moment, I think he took my indulgence and forgiveness for granted, even when I lost my temper. But the one thing he couldn't bear was to be shunned by his dearest friend. From then on, I used this method judiciously, though its effect diminished over time.

Up to this point, Caleb no doubt assumed that he was the main man in my life. Well, he was, as long as Joe remained at sea. While my husband was away, I emailed him updates on the donkey's latest antics. Sharing Caleb stories, he wrote back, made him the most sought-after man on board the ship.

As soon as Joe came home, we caught up with each other's lives. Our far-flung field assignments had required lengthy separations — but, as two autonomous people marrying late, we had found a way to make our long-distance relationship work. After a few days of wining and dining, romance and storytelling, I asked Joe, "So, do you want to meet the beast?"

"Sure. Let's go over," he said with a grin on his wind-beaten face.

On the six-mile drive to Silver Rock, I gave Joe a crash

course in animal communication. As he was probably the biggest, tallest man Caleb would ever meet, I was worried. "Move slowly, and don't approach him face-on," I said. "No sudden movements of your hands. Keep them low. Eyes down. No staring. Speak in a low voice." Above all else, I didn't want their first impressions of each other to be negative. Though Joe's opinion might evolve over time, Caleb's probably wouldn't. Joe nodded, half listening, not taking me seriously. I steered the car into Silver Rock's driveway and parked.

Around the corner from the stall, I told Joe to stay out of sight until I led the donkey out. When I had buckled the halter on and tied the lead line to the wall, I said, "Okay, Joe. Come on over."

Joe charged around the corner at a fast lope, aiming straight at the donkey's face. Not a good idea, even for people Caleb knew well. When Joe was a foot away, he grabbed Caleb's muzzle and encased his head in some sort of armlock. He began rubbing the knuckles of his free hand — hard — up and down the astonished donkey's bony forehead. He was giving him a noogie! I rushed forward to intervene.

Ignoring me, Joe said in a loud voice, "How's the man, Caleb? Eh, buddy?"

The effect astonished me. Caleb, after tossing his head attempting to free himself, relaxed, and his ears popped straight up. When Joe released him, the donkey gently head-butted him on the chest and made the same grunting, snuffling sounds he made when I first met him.

"He likes you!"

I should have known. Since I'd met Joe, I had witnessed the inexplicable effect he had on animals and children, especially "difficult" ones. Never having had kids or pets of his own, Joe was a magnet for both. Toddlers climbed into his lap and nested there. In fact, I first dated him because he was the only male my scarred old tomcat, Otto, would come near. When Otto first jumped up on his lap and batted at him, I wondered about the inner depths of my quiet neighbor.

Still, I was amazed by Joe's method of greeting Caleb — giving him a noogie, or what his family called a "Dutch rub" — and even more so by the donkey's enthusiastic response to the rough gesture.

"Can I walk him?" Joe asked. I untied the line and handed it to him. As soon as I let go, Caleb loped off toward the dressage ring with his new playmate in tow. Joe braced his feet forward and slid through the gravel, trying to stop the runaway. I waited for the inevitable trip-up when Joe would flop forward into the stance Lou Bridgman aptly dubbed "face skiing." But Caleb had met his match. His new human buddy wouldn't let go. Instead, Joe inched his way up the rope until he was neck and neck with Caleb. Next, he grabbed the donkey's muzzle in a headlock and gave him another noogie.

"What are you trying to do? Wrestle him to the ground?" I yelled as I caught up with them.

Joe had no desire to ride Caleb, but he frequently came along to stroll around the stables with us. When pain from my old back injury asserted itself, he would help me clean Caleb's flying, kicking hooves. Although Caleb was more docile with my husband than with me and seemed to accept him as a buddy, Joe's arms, like mine, sported lots of bruises from the donkey's playful nips and kicks.

This affection didn't extend to interhuman displays of affection, though. If I hugged Joe or even just touched him, Caleb's ears flattened against his head, and he snorted like a steam engine until we gathered him into the middle of the huddle. Did he want to protect Joe, his new buddy, from unwanted cuddling? Or was he jealous when I showed affection to someone other than him? My guess was the latter.

After two months of shore leave, Joe had to return to the ship. This time he carried photos of Caleb and boasted a bunch of new stories about the big donkey.

CHAPTER 13

Caleb Meets the Farrier

OUR FIRST ENCOUNTER WITH THE FARRIER, a.k.a. "the horse-shoe guy," occurred two months after Caleb's arrival at Silver Rock. I went into the dim barn to introduce myself to Stewart Strauss. Several horse owners told me they were intimidated by this apparently cantankerous man. At first, all I could make out in the gloom was the huge rump and floor-length tail of a white draft horse named Oscar, the biggest horse at the stable. At that moment his dinner-plate-size hoof rested in the lap of a kneeling man. From the back I studied this wiry person in jeans, a plaid flannel shirt, and a leather apron. Finally I said, softly, so as not to startle them, "Hi, I'm Margie Winslow. I'm the one with the donkey."

Still holding the hoof, Stewart turned his head to reveal a long and narrow face, with hollow cheeks and an eagle beak of a nose bent slightly to starboard. His face could have been carved in granite on some moldering tomb dating to the Crusades. Other than the addition of a gas-fired forge bolted to the bed of his pickup truck, the tools and methods of hoof care apparently hadn't changed much since then. In answer to my greeting, he spat a stream of tobacco juice into a dark corner. "Lift up, damn you. Come on now, lift it up!" I jumped back, thinking he was yelling at me. He looked over his shoulder again and said in a dry, nasal voice, "Watch them hooves." From where I stood three feet away, it looked like Stewart was directly in line for a knockout punch from a hoof, not me.

I waited until Stewart released the heavy hoof from his lap, letting it drop with a steely clang. While he adjusted his position, a semi-kneeling squat, to pick up the next hoof, I quickly asked, "Do you trim donkey hooves? Mine doesn't need shoes." Caleb had never worn shoes, and the Bridgmans said that he didn't need them unless we planned to be on pavement most of the time.

"Yeah," he said. "I've done a few donkeys. Kickers, you know." He stood up and ran a muck-stained hand through his curly gray hair. "And they can kick any leg in any direction. You know what a cow kick is? Well, donkeys and mules can kick their legs sideways — even two legs at once! Fast and hard! Most farriers won't touch 'em."

"Yes, I heard that. But mine has had his hooves trimmed all his life." On the other hand, I'd never looked up his previous "pedicurists" to see if they still had their front teeth. Or whether their noses were flat or bent.

"I'll look at him when I'm done here."

I trotted back to my car and retrieved one of several reference books with diagrams on proper hoof trimming for donkeys. A half hour later, I guided Caleb in and lined him up. Before Stewart crouched to begin his work, I showed him the pages with the instructions on how to trim a donkey's hooves. Stewart ignored me and picked up a brutal-looking pair of clippers.

After a few minutes, I just had to ask, "How are his hooves?"

Stewart stood up, holding his back. "Well, he's got one on each corner. Just like a table."

"A table with hooves?" I said, attempting to make the curmudgeonly man smile.

Without any sign that he'd heard me, Stewart said, "Hold him, can ya?"

Having no idea how to hold a large animal in place, I grabbed his long muzzle and squeezed. I whispered in his ear, "It's okay, Caleb. Hold on."

"*Hold him*, I said," Stewart called in a deep, muffled voice from a position beneath Caleb's tail, which smacked back and forth across the man's face. He cursed and spat another wad of wet tobacco onto the floor. I tucked Caleb's neck under my arm and tugged him forward until the crossties were taut. Maybe that would help.

A few minutes passed as Stewart applied a big metal rasp and sanded a hoof. He spoke in a friendlier tone: "Big one, isn't he? Sure he's not a mule?"

"Nope. He's all donkey," I said. It was a point of pride for me. No half-horse, half-donkey hybrid for me; nothing less than 100 percent pure donkey would do.

Stewart bent over to pick up the other hind hoof. "Argh. Did you see that? The son of a bitch — pardon my French — just about kicked my ear off! Hold him, damn it!"

"That one's his kicking hoof," I offered, aware of how lame I sounded. How holding the donkey — any part of him — short of hog-tying him, might control his hind legs, I had no idea. Perhaps I could turn his attention toward me. "No, no, Caleb. Be nice," I said, with all the authority of a field mouse.

Stewart knelt down and grabbed his leg again. This time he didn't relent as Caleb swung his hoof back and forth. The donkey's interest in the game ebbed after a few seconds, and he surrendered his foot to the farrier's lap. I watched the top of Stewart's head and narrow shoulders as he filed down the hard outer part of the hoof.

Suddenly, there was a loud crash of metal striking concrete. Stewart was sprawled against his tool cart. Just then Caleb's hind leg swooped out in a blur, Stewart jumped up, and the leg shot right between his thighs. From where I stood, it looked like a direct hit.

"Cut it out, you damned hunk of…dog food," he growled and thumped the donkey's flank. "You see that? Almost made me a soprano." He emitted a loud bark. "I call it 'the donkey handshake.'" Stewart was laughing!

He picked up the leg again and steadied it until Caleb gave up his struggle. Somehow, the farrier managed to clean and trim all four hooves, muttering the whole time.

After each trimmed hoof was firmly on the ground, he slipped a small cookie into Caleb's mouth. When he released the last hoof, however, no cookie appeared. As a show of finality Stewart flung the foot-long metal rasp across the stall, where it slammed into his steel-framed tool cart. The ordeal had taken the better part of forty minutes. Caleb tapped his left front hoof, the last one Stewart had trimmed, then stomped all four hooves, and finally aimed a swift kick at the tool cart, scattering steel tools and nails across the floor. Stewart pushed his thick glasses up his nose with a blackened finger. "I think the damn beast can count! He wants that last cookie!"

At this he smiled, revealing a mouthful of crooked teeth. He fished out a crumpled cookie from his battered cart and gave it to the eager donkey.

"Hmmph. He's not so bad," he said as he patted Caleb on the rump, "for a donkey."

CHAPTER 14

Donkey Dressage

I HAD JUST SPENT FIFTEEN MINUTES hustling Caleb toward the big ring when Laura hailed me from her office door: "Wait, Margie. We're working in the dressage ring today."

The dressage ring? *Dressage?* Although I was fascinated when I first watched highlights of the dressage competition from the Atlanta Olympics, I had never placed myself in the same saddle, so to speak. *Dressage*, as defined by the International Equestrian Federation, is "the highest expression of horse training," where "horse and rider are expected to perform from memory a series of predetermined movements." *Right.* As much as I tried to superimpose an image of Caleb on one of those dancing horses, I failed. Still, the only stable who'd welcomed us was our home. And the gorgeous ballet of dressage was Laura's specialty.

Why Laura thought that Caleb and I would do well at dressage when we could barely trace a circle was beyond me. For the last nine months, lessons with Laura three days a week had produced only microscopic improvements. Progress was impossible to gauge: some days Caleb seemed to understand what all the squabbling was about; other days he turned into a pillar of salt. Whenever I was irritable while grooming and tacking him, he kicked and nipped me; when I was impatient for him to move — especially if we were late — he planted his feet. But I was too preoccupied to notice that he mirrored my every mood.

Several times in the last month I had wondered if this was the worst possible time to take on a large untrained — possibly untrainable — animal. Right at that moment in my career what I needed most was relief from the tensions at work, not a new challenge. Even more so, I wanted to give and receive affection and find solace in a warm, calm companion, especially when Joe was away half the year.

So Laura wanted us to learn dressage? A new challenge? Dressage involves the perfection of subtle, even minute, cues — each squeeze of the rein or of the thigh, every shift in seat position signals a command to the horse. Even though I had no interest in entering a dressage show, I recognized that learning a few refinements might prove useful on the trail. So, while I harbored doubts about whether training for an elite sport would fit Caleb's or my personality, I kept my misgivings to myself.

Caleb and I entered the dressage ring. Right away I noticed one huge disadvantage: no fence. He could bolt to his nearby stall or plunge into the nearby flower beds.

"Our goal for the lesson," Laura called out, "includes twenty-meter circles and figure eights." Unlike Caleb and me, she was focused on the task. "Trace a diagonal from *M* to *K*."

The dressage ring was bounded by cone-shaped markers with a single capital letter on each one, but the letters, mysteriously, did not follow in alphabetical order. I swiveled to peer at each marker, looking for *M*. Twisting my hips in the saddle signaled Caleb to swivel with me. Without any coaching, he apparently understood what I had read were called "seat commands." I was amazed. The second surprise was that Caleb headed straight for the *M*, as if his eyesight was better than mine. As if he could *read*!

Laura pulled me back to the task at hand. "On the straightaway, go from *M* to *B*." I was still squinting at the markers in search of *B* when she continued, "Turn right at *B*, and proceed to *E*."

"*B* to *E*, *B* to *E*," I mumbled to myself. "Where the…?"

"At *E* turn left and follow *K* to *A* to *F* to *B*. Cut across to *E*. Turn right and finish at *C*. Got that?"

"Well, uh, not exactly," I said. I rubbed my neck, already sore from torquing left and right in search of the letters. It was hopeless. Caleb sensed my indecision and dashed out of the ring and straight into his stall with me still on board.

"Always dismount before entering a stall!" she shouted after us, as if I had planned our abrupt departure from the ring with this in mind.

During filming in Alaska and Chile for a PBS documentary about earthquakes, the director had observed that the quality of my unscripted statements peaked on the second attempt and deteriorated on every subsequent take. The camerawoman dubbed me "Two-Take Winslow." At least here I was in good company: Caleb's attention span seemed as short as mine, his boredom threshold set as low. *Two-Take Winslow meet Two-Take Caleb.* Since Laura worked with special-needs students, I began to wonder if maybe she had decided that *both* of us had ADD. Maybe we *did*.

Patience and persistence aside, Laura insisted on perfection from us. In line with English riding standards, she focused on the *rider*'s flawed arm, leg, and seat commands as the sole cause of an animal's misbehavior. More than once, she had said, "Caleb knows what to do." Sure, he *knew* what to do, but — even at the best of times — he only did what he *wanted* to do, *when* he wanted to do it.

At the next lesson and for several thereafter, she stopped us every few paces to fuss at me for my uneven hands or reins, for posting on the wrong diagonal (standing in the stirrups when I should sit, and vice versa), or for some other (to me) obscure reason. Constant stopping gave the donkey the impression that we never did anything for more than a few paces before Laura's voice would order: "Halt right there!" Like the smart donkey he was,

Caleb soon decided that taking a few steps and stopping was what we were trying to convey with all the yelling, kicking, and jerking of the reins.

At our next lesson, I begged Laura, "Could you let us continue if we're moving in even an approximation of the right direction until we have some momentum, at least?" Surely she had noticed that this donkey excelled at doing nothing whenever possible.

But no. To her, performing a move perfectly — with hands, feet, posture all correct — was paramount, so we continued for quite a few more lessons, never covering more than ten feet before Caleb would stop.

He was learning, all right, but not what we desired.

Several more weeks passed as Caleb and I battled for dominance. Oh yes, when it came to tenacity, this donkey had met his match. More than anything, what kept me coming back for lessons was that, as a high-achieving baby boomer, I, like Laura, always rose to a challenge. She and I had convinced ourselves, despite ample evidence to the contrary, that donkeys could do everything horses could do.

On a more basic level, I wanted — really needed — Caleb to obey me. But an uncomfortable question kept creeping into the foreground: *Will this donkey obey only when Laura wields the lunge whip?* In other words, would he submit to a person of authority, but not to me?

Nevertheless, Caleb had to be trained. No ifs, ands, or buts. As the Bridgmans had pointed out, a semitrained donkey like Caleb would be unwelcome at any stable. Besides, I wanted to ride him, preferably on trails. Having committed almost a year and many dollars into training this animal, I couldn't quit now.

CHAPTER 15

Donkey Gaits: Slow, Slower, and...Hold On!

"LET'S REPEAT THE PATTERN at a trot," Laura announced one morning in the ring. Her tone and energetic stride toward the dressage ring matched the brisk sunny day. I couldn't deny that Caleb could trot. Of course he could. On many occasions she had witnessed him pick up a lively trot toward the grain shed or one of the rosebushes on the property — usually with me in tow like a reluctant water-skier.

So, trot, *sure*. But tracing a neat pattern in the fenceless dressage ring at speed? What little steering control I had at the slowest walk swiftly devolved into complete chaos with an increase in pace. Any excuse I made, though, would fall on deaf ears. There was no stopping Laura when she had a plan.

With Laura as the irresistible force, I hoped that Caleb wouldn't act as the proverbial immovable object today. I feebly tapped his reluctant flanks. "Trot, Caleb." Laura raced over with the twelve-foot lunge whip snapping and chased us around the ring. Caleb's trot proved so bouncy that I couldn't read the letters on the posts. It felt like his chassis was set on square wheels or that his legs were all different lengths, or maybe enclosed in plaster casts. In the back of my mind, I suspected he was doing it on purpose, just to rattle my teeth. After a few more bounces, my glasses slipped off, and I had to stop and dismount to retrieve them.

Nevertheless, I followed Laura's orders and kept at it. What choice did I have? The carrot, so to speak, for me was the chance of going on a trail ride. The nearest equine trails were ten miles away, so we'd need to get there by trailer. So far, neither Laura nor any of the riders with trailers had invited us along. After watching us blundering around the ring or clogging the driveway, who could blame them? And Joe and Laura both insisted that we shouldn't buy a trailer to attempt solo excursions until I could safely handle my steed.

As if basic dressage at a walk and trot didn't create enough of a challenge, a few weeks later Laura asked me, "Do donkeys canter?"

I stalled her, saying, "Not that I know of. I'll look it up." I dreaded the very thought of even more speed with the inevitable loss of control. After all, part of the reason I had bought a donkey was the oft-quoted phrase of donkey experts: "Donkeys have two speeds: slow and slower." I hoped that Laura would forget about it.

At our next lesson, however, she already had a plan. She told me to pick up a fast sitting trot on a tight turn, turn Caleb's head toward the outside, kick the inside leg, and call: "Canter!" So that he might get the idea, I hummed the three-beat tempo of *William Tell Overture*: "Da-da-dum, da-da-dum, dada, dum, dum, DUM!" Sure enough, the donkey did it! Caleb's canter, however, resembled a dolphin swooping straight up and straight down — not the gentle rocking rhythm of a horse. I wasn't sure if his headlong flight across the ring fell within any known category of gait — maybe a three- or five-beat bunny hop? Turning was impossible; my only option was to hang on as he dashed across the ring and then exited altogether. Instead of running to his stall, he dashed between the barns and down the driveway. Laura ran after us, shouting, "Whoa, halt!" as if it would make any difference. What did halt him just before he reached the busy road was a vehicle blocking the narrow lane.

Caleb stopped short and snorted at the big truck. Laura caught up and grabbed his bridle. Her sensible advice — "Next time, turn him before he escapes the ring" — fell on two pairs of deaf ears. As she walked off I managed to say, "Laura, could we put off cantering unless we're in the big ring?" I wanted a solid barrier between us and moving vehicles and pedestrians. Laura, I'd noticed, didn't usually welcome advice, especially if it might be interpreted as criticism. Another pair of deaf ears.

As I led Caleb from his stall for our next lesson, I was surprised when Laura said we were working in the big ring. *Hallelujah! Fences.* It was still quite early in our training with Laura, so this small victory felt sweet.

Laura, however, had a brand-new challenge in mind. She laid several four-inch-wide PVC tubes ten yards apart. First, she told us to walk over them. After a few balky moments while Caleb sniffed the tubes, he stepped over them without breaking stride. The next few lessons, we increased our pace until he could trot right over them without tripping.

Next, Laura mounted the tubes on four-inch mounts. Caleb's approach to the higher jumps was a bit unusual: He would trot right up to the low jump, slam on the brakes, and drop his head to sniff at the tube. Or else he played chicken with me and veered at the last second and trotted off toward the exit gate. A few times he head-butted the jump rail until it toppled.

Yet, despite his creative interpretation of the rules, Caleb soon grew to love jumping, almost as much as he liked knocking the flimsy structures over.

During our jumping lessons, Laura introduced the half seat. In preparation for the jump, the rider stands up in the stirrups until her seat is just above the saddle. This shifts her weight toward the front legs, her upper torso over the horse's neck in anticipation of the rear legs lifting off. Caleb soon mastered the low jumps, though he "popped" them

— that is, he tilted onto his hind legs, his torso rearing back, and hopped over like a rabbit.

I was relieved when Laura agreed that attempting anything higher than six inches while carrying a tall, heavy rider would put unnecessary strain on his legs. With my long torso raising the center of gravity, the slightest fidget could throw him off stride at the worst possible moment. Donkey shock absorbers weren't designed for jumping. Nor were my nerves.

One day Caleb and I had just finished a lesson in the big ring and were tracing one last circuit around the far end when a deafening crash sounded right behind us. An industrial-size dumpster loader at the nursery next door had dropped its steel container. The shock alone nearly knocked me from the saddle, but Caleb responded first. All instinct, he leaped into the air and galloped straight toward a solid wood two-foot-high jump, the highest at the farm, one that only a few expert riders attempted. We had never planned to try anything higher than a few inches and definitely *not* at a gallop. Until that moment, I didn't even know that donkeys *could* gallop. One thing I believed I could count on with donkeys was their *slowness*. In fact, all the books I had read claimed that a frightened donkey doesn't bolt as horses do.

At that moment, Laura was fifty yards away, unlatching the gate to exit. She turned at the sound of the crash just in time to witness a terrified donkey and rider barreling straight at her. Over Caleb's thundering hooves, I dimly heard her shout, "Turn, turn! Turn him!" She was too far away to intervene. Besides, what could she do? She knew full well not to step into the path of a speeding animal. She swooped her arms to the right, then to the left, as if directing a renegade jumbo jet. "*Turn* him!"

Holding both reins in one hand, I pulled with all my strength and leaned far back in the saddle. *Nothing.*

Obsessed with escape from the metallic bomb blast, Caleb zeroed in on the jump. *Oh no! He can't jump it! He'll kill himself. He'll kill both of us!*

When Laura saw that I couldn't budge him from his trajectory, she raised her arms and swung them forward as if to make a swan dive. "Aim for the middle! Line him up. Aim for the middle!" she yelled. And for the first time ever, Caleb did just what she asked.

Then I heard: "Half seat! Half seat! Hold on!"

Half seat, half seat, what the heck is…? My mind went blank.

The jump loomed closer, twenty yards, fifteen yards… no turning back now, unless, unless, the donkey stopped dead, in which case I would catapult alone over the wooden rail, missile-like, and break my neck. My worst fear come to life.

At this speed, bailing out wasn't an option.

Ten yards…

Oh okay. "Half seat" meant to lean forward like a jockey, grasp the mane, raise the butt slightly off the saddle, and squeeze your thighs like a nutcracker.

Five yards, four, three, two...

In a semi–fetal position, I gripped, puckered, clenched, and sucked with muscles I never knew existed, attempting to glue myself to the saddle. Curled into a ball, I closed my eyes as he tilted onto his hind legs and launched himself into the air. We were airborne, but would his hind legs clear the rail? Or would we land hard on the bar and collapse in a pile of broken lumber and limbs?

With just a tap of his hind hoof, he cleared the rail. His forelegs touched down hard, throwing me onto his neck, but somehow I stayed on, falling back into the saddle just in time. Caleb veered toward the gate, as if all the hounds of hell were still on his tail. Laura stepped forward, her arms spread wide, and blocked our exit. Riders who were just entering the ring applauded, shouting, "Yay, Caleb!"

Ever the consummate teacher, Laura said in a some-what strained voice, "Okay, he overjumped it," meaning that he jumped higher than necessary. "And you overbalanced. Just don't try it again. Okay?"

As if.

CHAPTER 16

Whispering to Donkeys (or Not!)

AFTER A YEAR of ineffectually yelling, "Reins the same length! Hands the same height!" Laura agreed to seek out specialized help with Caleb. She and I had struggled for months to transform my rambunctious donkey into the perfect riding animal. But his blithe indifference to commands baffled even the usually unflappable Laura. To be fair, she was a certified dressage riding instructor, not a horse trainer, per se. In the middle of desperately wrestling my thick-necked charger to stop or turn, frankly I couldn't care less about the subtleties of the sport. If I would not, or could not, assume the role of alpha, as the Bridgmans and Laura demanded, I had to find another way to tame Caleb. And soon.

One day, Laura announced that her friend would introduce a new method of training to Silver Rock. As an avid reader, I already knew that a handful of horsemen and horsewomen had been teaching humane methods for thirty years. Sara, Laura said, had trained with one of them. Thinking more like Jane Goodall than General Patton, this new breed of trainer studied the subtle interplay of body language that wild horses use to establish dominance, show affection, and mete out discipline. They didn't "break" a horse in the traditional way, by breaking its will or its spirit through intimidation and bullying. Instead, they sought ways to "gentle" the horse, as they called it.

I knew already that donkeys were not herd animals, but I still wasn't clear how this social difference might affect training Caleb. The only donkey specialists I had interacted with, the Bridgmans, followed traditional horse-breaking methods.

The next time Sara came by the stable, I talked with her about our problems with Caleb. She took my concerns seriously. Laura must have discussed him already, because she said, "Oh yes. I heard." Eager to see what a new trainer with a new method might achieve, I signed up for six weeks of Sunday sessions.

On the first morning of class, Caleb was already braying at full throttle at the sound of my car. I hugged the snuffling beast and groomed him. On our way to the dressage ring, he marched eagerly, head-butting me the whole way, as if *I* were the one who needed prodding. Inside the ring we joined eleven horses and their young owners. Caleb swung his head left and right, curious about his fellow pupils. He butted my arm and nibbled his new lead line. I nudged him and mumbled, "Keep still." Once he had surveyed the setup, he rested his bony jaw on my shoulder. Hoping to keep him focused on me, I slipped him a cookie from my coat pocket.

Sara entered after me. The outfit she'd chosen matched a rather stiff demeanor: her long platinum-blond ponytail jutted out behind a precisely angled white cowboy hat; her tight pressed black jeans were tucked into shiny Western boots. Her first command was "Line up."

I shoved Caleb's chest back, then scurried around to the rear and leaned hard against his rump to shuffle him into rough alignment with the other horses. I, for one, was determined to put my best hoof forward.

Meanwhile, I strained to hear what the instructor said as she strutted back and forth along the line of attentive faces and muzzles. Wielding a long prod, Sara tapped the shoulder of one horse, the flank of another, to nudge them into a precise line. I had held the rod before class — while a nice carrot-orange color, its fiberglass shaft was as stiff as a golf club. To my mind, it masked a deadly weapon. The rod alone sparked my first misgivings about Sara's supposedly humane philosophy.

She returned to the first horse in the row, a placid chestnut. She didn't speak to the horse or touch him with anything other than her stick. As she proceeded down the line toward us, I whispered into Caleb's furry ear, "She may act like a Nazi, but she's just nervous."

Sara appeared out of nowhere and planted her pointy boots inches from my sneakers. She said, "Stop talking to him. Verbal commands are a waste of time."

I nodded meekly. Nevertheless, I talked to my donkey all the time. Books about donkeys and mules stated that the human partner's voice was *essential* for longears — especially in new situations or when they couldn't see you, such as when you're riding them. If most of my words were meaningless blather, as Lou Bridgman had implied, then why did Caleb always twist his foot-long ears toward my voice?

Meanwhile, Caleb jammed his nose into my side pocket. Sara spun around and demanded, "Have you got treats in your pocket?"

I could hardly deny it. Donkey slobber had already darkened the bulging pocket.

"Treats are totally distracting to him and to the other horses here."

"I'm sorry; you're right." I wondered where I could deposit the contraband without hauling the donkey off the field with me. As soon as Sara's back was turned, I stuffed the remaining cookies into his mouth.

Our instructor mercifully ignored her least promising students for the rest of the hour, and we slunk off to the barn as soon as class was dismissed.

At our next class, as Sara marched down the row of students and horses, they appeared to be backing up a few steps.

"We can do this, Caleb," I whispered.

The next thing I heard was a loud *thwump*. In the gap where his big head and neck should have been, a cloud of dust engulfed me. I turned to find him rolling on the ground, groaning and grunting loudly like a cow in a difficult labor. All four of his legs bicycled the air as he writhed back and forth. He rubbed his ears and cheeks against the ground, his big whiskery nose and lips quivering in ecstasy.

Bliss! (photo by Bruce Mason)

"Get him up! *Right now!*" Sara was back.

This animal weighs seven hundred pounds, lady. You get him up.

As if reading my mind, Sara asked me in a quieter voice, "How *do* you get him up?"

I looked down at his flailing hooves and suppressed a smirk. "I don't. He just gets up when he's ready."

Sara strode away, wisely choosing to ignore the troublemakers. She demonstrated some new technique to the next horse down the row.

Finished with his sand bath, Caleb stopped rolling and folded his legs under his belly and, with a loud grunt, heaved himself onto his feet. I stood facing front, in classic halter-class pose, bracing for the inevitable. A second later, he shook a pound of damp sand all over me. From his point of view, he was clean. I was filthy. *Score one for Caleb.*

Sara had been explaining something, which I had missed. She charged down the line to us, the dreaded Carrot Stick raised as if to strike us dead. She said, "Now you do it."

"Do what?"

Sara sighed and gazed at the ground. With exaggerated slowness, she grasped Caleb's lead line and jiggled it in front of his face.

She craned her neck toward an audience of fellow students and passersby and said, "Watch this. This will capture his attention. He'll raise his head up and step back in line."

She passed the line to me, and I jiggled the rope. It worked! He backed up. *Score one for the Method.* Once he understood the cue, he kept backing up. I joined the other students in jiggling their ropes, stepping their horses backward around and around the ring. This method was a great improvement over manhandling him. Caleb could back up forever. The class ended on a positive note. In his stall, we toasted our success with cookies.

The following Sunday, the donkey and I entered the ring ready to learn. When Sara joined the class, I pushed and shoved him back into line as fast as I could. (The jiggle method had stopped working the day after the last lesson.)

Caleb grabbed the rope and chewed on it. I didn't mind, as gnawing on his rope acted as a potent pacifier. Unfortunately, no donkey transgression proved too small to escape Sara's notice. The challenge Caleb and I presented apparently eclipsed the efforts of my classmates. She trotted up the line, zeroing in on us. She addressed the audience of kids and adults who sat in the grass outside the ring. "If you want your horse to stop chewing on the lead line," she announced in a loud, clear voice, "you can use reverse psychology." Echoes of Lou Bridgman.

Sara pointed at Caleb, whose eyes were half-closed as he munched blissfully. "He wants to put the rope in his mouth? Fine. Just feed him more line until he spits it out."

Sara snatched the rope from me. Standing next to the donkey's head, she crammed loops of wet, sand-encrusted rope into his mouth. Inch by inch, it disappeared into his willing maw. Caleb eagerly stretched his rubbery lips and arched his mouth wide to move the growing gob with his tongue to make more room for the next coil. From his pointed ears and bright eyes, I could almost read his mind. *I can do this. Everyone is proud of me.*

On the sidelines, people started to giggle. Sara accelerated her efforts, pushing larger coils into Caleb's drooling mouth. He tossed his head and laid his ears back but hoovered up the next inch of line with deft maneuvers of his tongue. *Was this supposed to be humane?* I looked between the rope remaining in Sara's hands and the short segment still lying on the ground. At least three feet of the sandy one-inch-diameter line — about the size of a cantaloupe — had dis-

Caleb's baleful expression during training (photo by Bruce Mason)

appeared, yet my donkey was still gamely tonguing another loop into his mouth. It dawned on me that he might choke or swallow sand and develop colic. *How many people did it take to perform a Heimlich maneuver on a seven-hundred-pound donkey? And where, exactly, was his diaphragm?*

Just as an objection bubbled up in my throat, Sara abruptly dropped the rope and turned on her heel. She stomped away, shaking her head and muttering, "He's impossible."

As soon as Sara's back was

turned, Caleb, with a guttural "GU-ROOSH," spewed the steaming mess right between her shoulder blades.

This time no one hid their laughter. But Sara possessed sufficient pride not to wipe the slime-soaked sand off the back of her white shirt. Head held high, she reached the end of the row and set forth to teach the next training technique.

I picked up the sodden line, trembling from the belly up, trying not to laugh out loud. *Score two for Caleb.*

Between two weekend field trips with my students and extra meetings at the college, I hadn't practiced as much as I had hoped. Nevertheless, I was determined to come away from the course with some techniques I could use. Maybe I would just chuck the sections that seemed unnecessarily aggressive, such as "friendly-ing the horse with the Carrot Stick." Leaving aside the new vocabulary words, the pricey props, and so on, weren't we still attempting to intimidate a large animal into submission? Then again, how else did an eighty-pound kid hope to control a half ton of equine muscle using a wimpy little piece of rope? At the same time, I couldn't help but sympathize with my donkey's rebellion against what was beginning to look, at least to me, like a sugarcoated form of bullying.

On the drive over to the stable for the next class, I considered our instructor's point of view. No one liked to be humiliated in public. Before I had acquired Caleb, I was especially sensitive to people laughing at me unless I deliberately brought it on myself. With my donkey, however, I had inadvertently cast myself in the role of eternal straight man. I hoped that, like me, she could learn from Caleb to take life a little less seriously.

At the stable, I groomed a sleepy, innocent-looking donkey before leading him toward the dressage ring. I said, "Caleb, let's not steal the show today, okay? Just do what she says for an hour. We can do that. Can't we?"

We turned the barn's corner and saw that the dressage ring was empty. Following the sound of excited voices, we merged with the other students leading their horses into the big ring, where a crowd of people were already jostling for room along the rails.

"Oh no." I sighed. "It's graduation day." I had forgotten. Today was the last class, though Caleb and I had yet to master even the first lesson. I guided him out onto the field and trotted to the far end, hoping Sara would ignore us. And she should have, for her own sake as well as ours. But as soon as we were lined up, she headed straight for us.

"Here she comes," I groaned under my breath.

Without preamble, Sara grasped Caleb's lead line. Holding the Carrot Stick in her other hand, she waved it up and down next to his shoulder and jiggled the rope in his face. The maneuver worked. He stepped back. I looked on with a modest smile.

She didn't stop there. With the line taut, she advanced

on him, stomping her feet, and backed him into smaller and smaller circles. His ears dropped back to warning position, but he kept backing away from the orange whirlwind spinning near his face.

"Go, Caleb," I whispered. Surely Sara was finished with the maneuver. Her least promising student had obeyed. So why did she continue to advance on him with the whirring stick and snapping rope? This must be one of the more advanced maneuvers taught on the days I missed. She pushed him into even tighter circles until he was tripping over his own legs. Cornered, he reared up, his rock-hard hooves punching the air over her head.

"Oh no!" I cried.

Caleb crashed down on all fours inches from Sara's toes and bolted, dragging her over to the fence, where some small kids perched. I pursued my snorting donkey, calling, "Whoa. Easy, boy. Easy."

The other students headed for the exit. Anyone could see that the donkey was confused and upset. Anyone, that is, except Sara. The donkey's ears were pinned flat against his head, and he was breathing hard and fast. His coat streamed with sweat. Alone with Caleb and me in the ring, she planted herself directly in front of him and swung the stick in faster, bigger arcs.

"Wait. Wait," I called out. I was paralyzed with indecision: Should I flee from the panicking donkey or stay in the ring? "Someone's going to get hurt," I told Sara.

She shouted at me, "Stay out of the way! You're making things worse." She advanced on him again, forcing him to back up. With the rope whipping back and forth like a crazed snake, he backed up several more steps, his eyes wide with fear. The moment I dreaded was close at hand.

In the space of a heartbeat, though, Caleb surrendered, but on his own terms. His knees buckled, and he sank to the ground. Rolling onto his side, he raised his head to look up at Sara with sad eyes. This time no one laughed.

Sara looked down at the sweaty, sand-caked mass and turned on me. "Get him up! Don't let him do this to you."

Do this to me?

We were all much safer with the upset animal on the ground, so I did nothing. But Sara wasn't finished. She whipped his hind legs with the stick — not feeble taps with the tassel but full-armed wallops using the shaft. "Get up! Get up!" she yelled.

Caleb flinched with each blow, swung his head left and right, but stayed down. His ears lay limp and askew on each side, like broken wings. Rage jolted me out of my frozen terror. I rounded his flank and grabbed the stick from Sara.

"Stop it!" I screamed in her face. "Stop hitting him right now!"

Sara and I locked eyes. In those few seconds, I saw something I hadn't noticed before: desperation. She dropped her gaze before I did, dropped the rope and stick on the ground, and strode toward the gate.

I looked down at my poor donkey. He stopped swaying his head from side to side and, with a loud sigh, laid his massive cranium in the dirt. There, in the middle of the ring under the watchful eyes of the onlookers, he closed his eyes.

I knelt by his head and said softly, "Come on, Caleb. Get up. Up. Let's go. We're finished here."

He rolled onto his chest, struggled to his knees, and heaved himself up onto his feet. I picked up the rope and led him out of the ring, his ears still at half-mast, both of us avoiding eye contact with the silent audience. I couldn't trust myself to speak.

Safely inside his stall, I touched the donkey's sweaty flank and realized he, too, was trembling. I sang and whispered sweet nothings in his ears as I toweled him down. I almost wept with relief that he hadn't turned on Sara or crashed the fence. In those few seconds of rising panic, this big, powerful animal could have trampled bystanders, including me. Or bolted off in a frenzy and broken his leg. I whispered to him, "But you didn't hurt anyone, my good boy. Did you?"

As if in response, Caleb pawed the ground, first slowly, then faster and faster. I leaned over and picked up his hoof. Failing to achieve a high five, I shook his heavy foreleg up and down. "Way to go, Caleb!"

CHAPTER 17

What Does a Donkey Want?

IT WAS HIGH NOON on a hot summer day. Caleb stood in the center of the big ring, staring at the far end, poised like a retriever. After the debacle with Sara and her new Method, Laura and I had resumed twice-weekly lessons in the ring. In between, I rode Caleb by myself in the ring or on one of the trails next to the stable. I came to cherish moments like these when I could spend time alone with him. Today, thankfully, we had the ring to ourselves, as most of the serious riders were away at a horse show.

Several Canada geese had landed next to a jump made of straw bales and were plucking at the bundles. Unlike a horse, which will spook at unexpected objects in the ring, Caleb was riveted by the unexpected visitors. He inched toward them and paused.

From what I had observed at the stable, the horses — when not totally passive — focused on other horses or their owners. Caleb, however, focused first and foremost on the natural environment. Donkeys in the wild, I had read, usually live semisolitary lives much like deer, except for mating or defending their young. Yet, unlike most prey animals, donkeys are curious and are drawn toward novelty rather than avoiding it. Absolutely anything commanded his attention — anything other than my commands.

Caleb advanced three paces and stopped again. As he assessed the situation, I gazed around the boundaries of the ring. If Laura appeared and saw us idling — and she seemed to pop up everywhere — she would bark out an order or three. "Gather the reins. Tap him with the crop…"

But I knew full well that there was no point in forcing his attention when he was like this. I could work up a sweat kicking and yelling, but he would ignore my cues. We were on Donkey Time. I could wait.

What is he thinking about?
(photo by Kjeld Tidemand)

But forced idleness carried my thoughts far from the ring to less relaxing concerns. The fall semester at City College had been particularly rough for me: I was balancing the heaviest teaching load in the department and mentoring more than my fair share of students. Worse, the confiscation of classrooms and labs had reached our department. Only that morning I had found the computer lab gutted, all the computers and furniture removed. My students and I had had to retreat to the library and somehow learn computer skills armed only with paper and pencil.

Caleb's analysis of the geese concluded, and he made his move. He picked up a brisk trot and ushered the geese off the field. Protesting, they took wing and soared over the treetops. Caleb seemed surprised by this magical ability. As I followed the birds' trajectory through the V of his poised antennae, my gaze settled on his jutting Neanderthal brow.

And that was when it suddenly hit me. The image of a Neanderthal resonated in a lot of ways as I thought about donkeys vis-à-vis horses. I had always held a soft spot in my heart for Neanderthals: those craggy-browed hominids who lost out around twenty thousand years ago to the more agile, more socially organized Johnny-come-latelies — the *Homo sapiens*. Scientists often assumed, wrongly, that Neanderthals were less bright than modern humans; after all, they had faded into extinction.

Just as Neanderthals were not a wannabe version of *Homo sapiens* as far as I knew, donkeys were not wannabe horses! Yet from the very beginning, this is how I had seen Caleb. Laura and the Bridgmans had, too. The little donkey that could. Ha!

When their genetic endowments are compared, of course, it's obvious that donkeys are not horses; horses possess 64 chromosomes, donkeys 62. Before assuming that superiority correlates with chromosome count, I recalled that modern humans have 46 chromosomes, gorillas 48, chickens 78, and goldfish 94. Has anyone ever saddled up a goldfish? So, what's missing in donkeys? Perhaps nothing at all, except maybe the follow-the-leader gene.

Up to this moment, I hadn't thought to ask myself: What was it like to be a donkey in a world of human expectations? Archaeological excavations by Fiona Marshall near Abydos, Egypt, revealed that donkeys were domesticated over five thousand years ago in North Africa. According to their bone structure, their stock came directly from the nearby African wild ass. They were the first beasts of burden and transport in Egypt, long before camels and horses. Not only that, but the Abydos site appears to contain the oldest evidence of a domestic animal honored after death. The careful burial of donkeys in neat rows near a king's grave pointed to their value. Compared with today's stubby Mediterranean breed, they were tall and graceful. I wondered how these magnificent beasts had been lured into service by humans. Protection from wild predators and a steady diet probably helped.

Donkeys, once domesticated, lost status to the larger, swifter horse — a native of central Asia — a thousand years later. In race or in battle, of course, the horse reigned supreme.

Donkeys, unlike horses, could survive on poor-quality straw, needed less water, and could work harder and longer under the brutal sun. They required so little care that, sadly, they received less. Although the history of domestication paints a bleak picture, some donkey stocks were carefully bred for size and grace, including the white Andalusian, ridden by the Moorish aristocracy, and the black Catalonian, the prize donkeys sent to George Washington as a gift from the king of Spain.

Unfortunately, the donkey's resistance to complete submission led to ill treatment. As I saw it, the little donkey's only way to avoid losing its spirit altogether and surrendering, as wild cattle and sheep had done long before, was to hold back a little independence. But many humans — whose lives were every bit as harsh as their animals' — equated the donkey's resistance, or "stubbornness," with stupidity. At least that was my take on it.

But the most significant difference between horses and donkeys derived from their social behavior. The horse, as a herd animal, is more amenable to subjugation by humans, who could exploit its instinct to follow a leader. When a horse was separated from the safety of other horses, the human handler could appoint him- or herself the leader.

As Farley Bridgman, following the tradition of "breaking" horses, had pointed out, the human had to be the alpha, not the animal.

I already knew that the wild donkeys of North Africa when faced with a new situation will freeze rather than flee like horses. So far, so good for this nervous rider. But I had also read that donkeys' second instinct is to face down and fight rather than yield to a challenge.

I knew most of this before I met Caleb. But how did the donkey's social behavior affect training? Although I had read that donkeys were not herd animals, when I looked up similar animals that live semisolitary lives — like deer, for example — I found no instances of anyone trying to train them. It wasn't the first time I had thought about this, but now it was becoming impossible to ignore.

Until now, my research about donkeys was overridden by wishful thinking. As an indulgent mother / pet owner of what I saw as my "noble steed," I was convinced that Caleb was unique, a genius. With consistent training, he could do anything. He'd already amazed people by opening latches, stealing hats, and barging in on pony parties uninvited.

While my thoughts ricocheted around my brain, Caleb had edged toward the gate and shook the chain latch with determination. After ten minutes of standing around while his rider was lost in thought, he'd clearly had enough of the ring. Frankly, so had I.

CHAPTER 18

Road Warriors

CALEB AND I continued with lessons as Laura's worst students for two more years. It was past time to think — and *be* — outside the box. Or the ring. Where could Caleb and I learn from each other without constant scrutiny? I spent the next week driving around the suburban neighborhoods within a two-mile radius of Silver Rock. On the county atlas, I marked where the roadside margins were wide enough for off-pavement riding. A mile and a half away from the stable stood hundreds of acres of the huge, mostly abandoned Rockland Psychiatric Center. A quick drive through revealed that, although the buildings were all boarded up, a public bus passed through the middle of the complex. I reasoned that if we stayed on the paved streets, no one would force us to leave.

One sunny summer morning, after Joe had been home from his latest trip for a week or so, I had an idea. "Are you up for an adventure?"

When he was home from the sea, Joe often showed willingness to aid and abet in what he referred to as my "wacky schemes." I tried an indirect approach. "Do you think Caleb would follow you if you pedaled your bicycle out onto the road?" If Caleb followed a leader, I reasoned, the donkey's focus would remain fixed on his buddy, not on passing cars or windblown trash, which he found so terrifying.

Joe and I debated the pitfalls, but in the end, he agreed. On the morning of our experiment, he loaded his old red bicycle into the back of our van, and we drove over to the stables. Once Caleb was groomed and tacked, I mounted him and rode up the driveway behind Joe's bike. When we reached the road without a single mishap, I said to Joe, "Let's aim for the psych center."

Joe stood on the pedals and tore off. Caleb pounded up the pavement after him, ears pinned flat, in hot pursuit.

"Oh no! Slow down, Joe!" I yelled at his retreating back.

The deep rumble of a big diesel engine warned me that we were not alone. I turned to look back over my left shoulder to check. The slightest twist of my torso Caleb interpreted as a left turn, and he veered straight into the path of the speeding truck. The monster vehicle swerved around us without slowing and sped off, the driver honking and shaking his fist. I wrenched Caleb over to the side and stopped. Several minutes passed before my heart rate slowed to normal.

Caleb, his ears straight up and facing forward, concentrated on his goal: to catch up with Joe's bike, which waited for us two blocks away. As soon as I loosened the reins, he shot forward — right down the double yellow lines marking the center of the narrow road. In a panic, I tugged the reins so hard that he reared, almost dumping me. I said in my lowest voice, "Slow down, boy. Eeeeasy, ohhh-kaaaay. Attaboy," as if *he* was the one who needed to calm down.

When we caught up to the bicycle, Joe's torso was bent over the handlebars as he gasped for breath. Caleb sauntered up alongside him and slobbered on his shoulder, nibbled his ear, and — despite having been swatted away several times — nearly tore the bike's saddlebag off.

"Knock it off, damn it," Joe muttered, swatting him with his hat.

"Are you okay?" I asked.

"More or less."

After we caught our breath, I said, "You've got to slow down. We shouldn't be galloping down the road like this."

"Easy for you to say. You should have seen the look in those eyes. Caleb's wacko!"

"No, he's not. He's just enthusiastic."

After a few minutes of rest, while Caleb grazed among the wildflowers on the verge, Joe pedaled off again. At the sight of his departing back, the donkey's head snapped up and he accelerated like Seabiscuit charging through the gate at Pimlico.

Joe yelled over his shoulder, "Can't you slow him down or stop him?"

I yelled, "*You* slow down" — gasp — "then *he'll* slow down!"

"Slow down? With that monster coming after me? Forget it."

I tugged on the reins. *Nothing.* In the big ring, I often sought in vain for Caleb's gas pedal; outside the fenced enclosure, I had a runaway train.

Joe slowed down at an intersection, which allowed Caleb to barrel right into him. His front legs advanced until he had straddled the still-rolling rear wheel, tickling his chest hairs. He bucked a little at the new sensation but continued to inch forward until his belly cleared the back wheel, pushing Joe over the handlebars.

"Oh God, Joe. He's trying to *mount* the bike!"

Joe removed one hand from the handlebars and elbowed Caleb's chest, but he kept on coming, even when Joe yelled and smacked the donkey's nose with his hat.

"He *is* mounting it!" I said. Did he think the red bicycle was a mare?

Caleb ignored Joe's elbows and flapping hat and moved forward until his front leg rubbed against a pedal, which finally brought the whole circus to an abrupt stop. Just then a large panel truck passed, making a wide detour around us. The driver was treated to the sight of a man hunkered down over the handlebars of his red bicycle with a huge white furry mass riding his back fender — and a red-faced rider sitting on top of the whole pile.

Joe shoved Caleb's chest with one hand, while I backed him off the bicycle fender. My husband dismounted. Holding the handlebars with one hand and swinging his cap at Caleb's intrusive nose with the other, he pushed the bike down the road. The donkey trotted next to his elbow like a faithful dog, until he suddenly veered into Joe, knocking him and his bike to the ground. Joe got up and inspected a new tear in his shirt.

"Are you okay?" I asked. Joe gave me a wan thumbs-up but avoided eye contact. He righted his bike and turned to walk ahead.

"What scared you, Caleb?" Out of the corner of my eye I saw a yellow plastic bag flapping from a garbage can. "Come on. Easy, now. It's just a plastic bag, silly!"

Calmed by my words or maybe just tired, he turned his attention to the weeds on the shoulder of the road. A psychedelic-colored Hula-Hoop lying in a driveway set him off again, dancing sideways, snorting, and edging his rear end into the roadway.

Meanwhile, delivery and utility trucks, SUVs, and luxury cars raced past, as if we were invisible. I was shocked that there were so many vehicles on the road. Instead of slowing down to give us time to step off the pavement, their drivers gunned their engines and honked. Didn't they know any better? Instead of warning us off the road, the sudden noise threatened to create a rodeo right in front of their hoods.

We continued onward. As long as Joe stayed not too far ahead, I could arm-wrestle Caleb back into line again. Whenever he stopped to sniff something, I released the reins to relax my aching arms. Subjects of avid concentration included a hamburger wrapper, a yapping dog, and a dead squirrel. I rested while he devoted minutes of rapt attention to these novel treasures.

Forty-five minutes later we arrived at the poison ivy–shrouded gates of the old psychiatric center, setting a new donkey speed record of a mile and a half in thirty minutes. At least we had gotten this far more or less in one piece. I asked Joe, "Do you want to go inside?"

"Some other time," Joe said in a neutral voice. "We've got to get the Beast back home on the same roads, don't we?"

"How about for just a few minutes? There's no one around."

If there is one place spookier than a psychiatric hospital to me, it's an abandoned psychiatric hospital. So, why was I steering my donkey through its rusty gates? The setting was restful, with just the sound of late-summer crickets and the echoes of Caleb's unshod hooves rebounding off the massive soot-covered yellow-brick buildings. Ivy and Virginia creeper had all but gobbled up the facades. Rusted, ivy-covered meshed windows were opaque with grime, the doors boarded up.

As creepy as the ruins struck me, Caleb ignored them, his eyes myopically scanning the ground. That is, until he approached a large manhole cover. He reared over it, doing an exaggerated, comical double take — I expected his eyes to pop out on springs. After wrestling the panicky donkey back onto all fours, I studied the psychiatric hospital's dirty pebbled-glass windows concealed behind corroded steel mesh. What must it have been like to be confined, sometimes for years, behind these walls?

The paved streets of this city of the formerly damned were laid out in a neat grid, with stop signs, crossing stripes, and even street signs with pleasant names, like Oak and Maple. Benches dotted open lawns, shaded by fine old trees. Instead of a place of unspeakable horrors, this leafy campus must have been a welcome refuge for many.

I had settled into Caleb's loping donkey gait, when he stopped dead and pranced sideways next to yet another manhole cover, snorting at it like he alone could keep it from rising up to release a plague of donkey killers. Joe had stopped a few yards ahead to catch his breath, examine the torn sleeve of his favorite shirt, and wipe the sweat from his face. Caleb required some help to pass the gurgling monster. The storm drain, not Joe. I waited until Joe's shoulders straightened again before saying, "Can you goose him from behind?"

"*Goose* him?" Joe's red face and bulging eyes suggested something other than eagerness to comply. He counted to ten and then looped behind us. I waited, but Joe had stopped.

I yelled, "*Go!* Push him!"

Joe glided the bike forward a few inches until the front wheel passed right between Caleb's hind legs. With his rump level with Joe's head, Caleb raked his tail across Joe's face. Joe yelled and whacked him with his cap, at the same time backing up his bicycle as fast as possible. Caleb, however, backed up faster than Joe did, but he lost his footing and sat down hard on the handlebars. With my kicks and Joe's swats urging him on, Caleb regained his footing and, with a jump, escaped the ticklish wheel. We left the manhole monster behind.

Soon it became clear that as long as Joe's bike remained no more than twenty feet ahead of us, Caleb more or less sauntered past manhole covers and storm drains — which seemed to be spaced about fifty feet apart — hardly breaking stride.

Joe decided to turn left and pedaled up a gentle hill on a side street. This less-traveled street of broken pavement, with grass growing up between the cracks, might be off-limits to outsiders, but no one seemed to be around. Two blocks farther ahead, though, at the intersection with another shady street, I saw that about a dozen adults stood on the sidewalk in front of a building. "Whoa, Caleb," I said.

Joe noticed them, too, and said, "The place is supposed to be closed down, isn't it?"

"I thought so."

He turned his bike and coasted back down the hill. I turned Caleb to follow, but halfway through a wide U-turn in the middle of the street, he spied another manhole cover. He froze. He sniffed it, snorted. This was not just any manhole cover but the entrance to the underworld. He arched his back and started to buck.

"Easy, now, Caleb. Easy," I said in a low voice as I struggled to keep my seat. A fall onto cement pavement would be serious.

I hoped that the people were too far away to notice the dancing white donkey. Here was one time I dreaded Caleb's ability to attract strangers.

Out of the corner of my eye, I saw someone sprinting toward us clad in pajamas, a terry-cloth robe, and slippers. There were inpatients here, after all. The man stumbled and slowed, tripped up by the belt of his trailing robe, but continued to approach. Half a block away, he raised his arms in a gesture of…what? Supplication? Horror?

"Caleb, let's *go!*" I kicked harder and hauled hard on the right rein. "Move on! *Now!*" What would the patient do when he reached us? More important, might Caleb, already panicked by the gurgling monster under the iron lid, trample the man?

The man reached the curb and fell to his knees, his

look ecstatic, like a child gazing up at the Virgin at Lourdes. Caleb paused middance and raised his head to stare at the man, the manhole cover forgotten. The patient spoke up: "Excuse me, but, um, are you real?"

Astonished, I stared at the middle-aged man in his biblical striped brown-and-tan robe, kneeling a few yards away. For a second, I wondered if *he* was real.

In the distance, I noticed that a burly man in green scrubs had separated from the group and was trotting toward us. He was still too far to intervene.

The patient spoke again. "Are you really there?"

Caleb listened, one ear fixed on the kneeling patient, the other rotated 180 degrees to catch my answer. Speaking in a calm voice for the benefit of both man and beast, I said, "Hi! I'm Margie, and this is my donkey, Caleb." I patted the donkey's shoulder and smiled.

The man, still on his knees, giggled. "Oh, okay, that's good to know."

"Do you want to touch him?" I asked.

The man frowned and curled his hands into fists. "No. It's just…"

The orderly was twenty yards away and closing in fast. "You see," the patient continued, "sometimes I see things that aren't there."

"Oh yes. The donkey and I are real," I assured him, sounding like the Virgin in the grotto herself.

Just then, the orderly caught up and placed his hands

on the man's shoulders, gently for someone capturing an escaped patient. He helped the man to his feet and turned him away with a quick nod to me. Looking back over the attendant's shoulder, the patient said, this time in a childish voice, "Bye-bye, now. Bye-bye."

"Goodbye," I called. "Happy to meet you." And then, like an idiot, I called out after them, "Have a nice day."

With Caleb unstuck from the manhole, I jerked the right rein to turn him away from the departing patient and toward Joe, who had turned around and was pedaling back up the hill toward us. When he was close enough to hear, I whispered, "Did you see that?"

Joe lifted a weary leg over the bike seat, dismounted, and leaned the bike against a light post. He slowly wiped his glasses on a less-smeared section of his undershirt. In the meantime, Caleb stretched his neck over to the bicycle and sniffed its seat with disturbing thoroughness. Satisfied, he rested his heavy chin on it, closed his eyes, and sighed. His reverie was interrupted when the bike toppled over. Caleb stood over it, blinking.

"You mean that guy in pajamas? Yeah, I was wondering what you were doing there so long."

"He's a patient. He wanted to meet the donkey."

Joe, whose collar and shirt were torn, his back covered in slobber, and his legs and bike plastered with mud, didn't exactly look sane, either. "We'd better get out of here before security catches up with us."

As we rode down the main street, side by side, I recounted the odd conversation I'd had with the patient. Joe laughed a little and shook his head, no doubt in sympathy with him. "If the poor guy tells his shrink that he saw a big white donkey today," he said with a dry chuckle, "I'll bet they'll up his meds!"

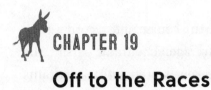

CHAPTER 19

Off to the Races

BY THE FOLLOWING FALL, Laura couldn't help but notice that our floundering efforts at dressage traced a downward trajectory. Boredom tumbled after frustration in a race to the bottom. At one of our lessons, seemingly out of the blue, she announced, "I think Caleb and you need a new challenge."

We hadn't even mastered our first one. Not really, but I waited to hear about what new ordeal she had in mind.

"I want you and Caleb to prepare for the hunter pace at Pound Ridge."

"A hunter pace? What is that?" Visions of red-coated riders galloping after hounds sprang to mind. Tallyho and all that.

"Look it up and we'll talk," she said.

I discovered that a hunter pace is a six- to ten-mile cross-country race through varying terrain, with intermittent jumps. *Jumps?!* Ahead of race day, members of the sponsoring riding club ride the course and record a slow time, a fast time, and an average. The times — like the length of the course — are kept secret until all entrants finish. (Or give up?) On race day, the rider who finishes the course closest to the average time, above or below, is the winner. So "the race is not to the swift." I liked this biblical concept.

As the date for the hunter pace drew near, however, dread knotted my stomach. I approached Laura and asked, "Are you sure this hunter pace is a good idea?" Foremost on my mind was the memory of the horse that years ago had spooked in the woods and thrown me over his head.

She waved me off, but when I asked about the jumps, she set my mind at ease: "There are go-arounds at each jump, so you can skip them." Laura added, "Mary Lee will be 'ponying' you on the pace. She'll stay with you and guide you through the course."

I didn't know Mary Lee any better than any of the other "boarders," as Laura called us. We were both professionals — she was a pediatrician — and about the same age. Mary Lee nodded when I said hello but, like all the serious riders, otherwise ignored me. I understood: Caleb and I blundered around the ring, cutting off riders and breaking equipment. I could almost read their minds: *There goes the weirdo with the donkey.*

In the plus column, I had often watched as Mary Lee rode Oscar, who was part draft horse, part Arabian. He was haughty, fierce, and huge. He looked like a medieval knight's charger, heavy enough to carry a soldier in full armor, and more than ready to plow through a whole army of Saracens. If anyone would keep us moving, Mary Lee riding Oscar would ramrod us through.

On race day, as I groomed and saddled Caleb, I remembered the mayhem he had caused among Silver Rock's horses and ponies when he first arrived. A few of them still bolted and threw their riders at the sight of him. "Forget about me, God," I prayed. "Just don't let us cause an accident."

Soon Laura was urging us to load. I couldn't resist asking her, "Isn't showing up at a hunter pace with a donkey kind of like entering a yacht race with a rowboat?"

Laura reassured me with a pat on the shoulder. "You'll be fine."

Oscar's stately form, all 1,700 pounds of him, clumped up the ramp of Mary Lee's trailer. As we closed the ramp and doors behind Caleb, the donkey torqued his helicopter-blade ears toward Oscar, who calmly chomped on some hay. Caleb followed suit.

I climbed into the cab and aimed for an enthusiastic note: "Off to the races!" Mary Lee bit her lip and stared straight ahead. Apparently, she wasn't pleased with her teammates. Six two-horse trailers from Silver Rock followed us up the highway and across the Tappan Zee Bridge. Forty minutes later, we entered a big field where dozens of other horse trailers were parked. All around us riders adjusted saddles and bridles and exercised their horses to stretch their legs.

Hunter pace at Pound Ridge, New York (photo by Laura Butti)

A few minutes later, Laura brought over our numbered pinnies to slip over our clothes. "Number 56. Wow, now we look serious!" I looked around for another donkey, or even a mule. Among over one hundred huge Thoroughbreds, Arabians, and warmbloods, not a single pair of long ears pierced the sky. At last, I spotted two fat Icelandic ponies ridden by girls wearing jeans and hairy Icelandic sweaters. Maybe we could keep up with *them*.

To avoid traffic jams on the narrow trails, I learned, teams of two set out at three- to five-minute intervals. Laura had registered our team for an early start time so we would have plenty of time to finish. We followed Oscar toward the ill-defined start area, where several volunteer race officials held stopwatches and clipboards. In the crowd of eager horses, Caleb was barely able to contain himself. He circled and pawed the ground, bent on catching up to the horses that had started before us. I wasted precious energy circling him back into line.

Soon we received a nod from the official with a stopwatch and clipboard. Caleb raced into the woods ahead of Oscar, scrambling over the slippery rocks to catch up with the team ahead of us. In seconds, Oscar's steaming nostrils nudged the donkey's skinny butt, and Mary Lee passed me in a wide spot. She drawled over her shoulder in a faint Kentucky accent, "You'd better keep up." And that was about all she said for the rest of the long day.

The donkey was forced to trot fast just to keep up with Oscar's sedate stroll. "'Keep up,' she says!" I muttered at the donkey's bouncing head. "Are you kidding?"

Oscar dashed ahead to the first jump and cleared it easily. Mary turned Oscar around and waited for us. Impatient with our slow pace, she lined Oscar up and vaulted the jump in the reverse direction, turned, and then jumped it again.

Caleb, inspired by Oscar's triple performance, sped up. Except for that *National Velvet* moment when Caleb had fled the dumpster months earlier, we had never cleared more than a six-inch jump. This one, easily two feet high, was made of double rows of straw bales. "Oh no, Caleb!" With hard jerks and kicks, I steered him around it.

Rounding the next bend, Caleb picked his way carefully around sharp rocks and mud, following Oscar's rapidly retreating rump. Every few minutes, Mary Lee reined Oscar in to wait. He snorted and pawed the ground, acting out his impatience on his rider's behalf.

About a half hour into the race, a traffic jam ahead revealed a pileup of a dozen or so horses backing up and refusing to cross a wooden bridge. Instead of waiting his turn, Caleb plowed through the crowd. He stepped onto the slimy wooden deck and trotted across the bouncing bridge like a champ. Meanwhile, several horses panicked at the sight or maybe the smell of the donkey and bolted off the trail into the swampy woods, their enraged riders cursing as they struggled to rein them in.

"Oops! Sorry about that!" I waved as we hurried past. Now we were ahead of a dozen horses. "Way to go, honker-donk!"

As soon as we were safely past, muddy horses and their riders scrambled back onto the path. A minute later, they all galloped by, making a wide detour around us.

All morning, late-starting teams passed us. I soon retreated into "just-keep-moving mode" despite pains in my knee joints and butt from gripping my wide-backed mount like a nutcracker. Eventually I was too tired to be terrified of falling off a stumbling donkey. Whenever other teams passed us, Caleb trotted or cantered a few steps, as his equine pride demanded. But as soon as the other horses vanished around the next bend, he slowed to a pace not much more animated than his on-his-way-to-the-glue-factory shuffle.

On the downslope into a shallow valley I perked up at the sight of cars, tables, people, and horses milling about. "We're done!" Caleb picked up on my renewed energy and trotted down to join the crowd.

Mary Lee burst my bubble. "It's the halfway point. Vet check."

Volunteers recorded the time of our arrival and scheduled a time-out. The vet in a white coat came over and placed her stethoscope against Caleb's fuzzy breast. She smiled and said, "We heard that there was a donkey coming along."

"I'll bet you did," I said. I could imagine the reports from enraged, muddy riders from the bridge crossing. After a quick rub of his neck, she said, "His heart rate is up, and he's drenched in sweat. Better let him rest for ten minutes."

Caleb and I were glad to comply, even though it forced Mary Lee and Oscar to linger, too. I didn't dismount — I was afraid my stiff knees and aching hips wouldn't cooperate if I attempted to remount. Volunteers offered slices of apple and water, which we four devoured. "Gee, we've done three or four miles in…what? An hour and a half?" I said to Mary Lee. She looked away.

"He thinks we're done," I said to a police officer who stroked the donkey's velvety muzzle. The insignia on his uniform indicated that he was part of a mounted police unit. He smiled and said, "Never saw a donkey at one of these races." I hoped that no complaints would reach his office.

When our ten minutes were up, I urged my steed into the woods behind Oscar. Caleb spun around and gazed longingly at the vet stop. "Hey! Treats back this way! You know: *T-R-E-A-T-S!*" he seemed to say.

Meanwhile, Mary Lee and Oscar started to attack the long slope of a major hill. I kicked, thrashed, and yelled until we were finally out of view of the vet station with its now-smirking volunteers. I figured that once he lost sight of the rest station, he would try to catch up with Oscar. But his hooves suddenly grew deep roots, and he even ignored the horses passing us. To his credit, we had already gone farther and faster than he and I had ever ridden before. There was nothing for it but to dismount. I limped up the hill in my stiff high-heeled riding boots, leading him by his reins. Caleb trotted along gamely at my shoulder, nipping my sleeve. "Aha! Better with the weight off, eh?" I puffed and grumbled as I towed him up the slope, not knowing — or even caring — if this disqualified us.

After a few minutes of steady trudging, I led him over to a tree stump and remounted. A few feet farther up the trail, though, he planted his feet again. No amount of yelling, whipping, or kicking made any difference. I dismounted. But this time he wouldn't budge. I leaned back on the reins and applied the whip to his flank. Two women riders on their gleaming horses passed us. As late starters, they must have galloped to catch up, but their horses didn't look at all winded. One rider called, "Is everything okay? Is one of you hurt?"

"No." I sighed. "We're just having a donkey moment."

They laughed and pranced up the slope. Caleb suddenly decided to follow them. I could barely keep up. If I dropped the reins, he might finish the race without me. Or, just as likely, veer back downhill to the vet station and the treats.

When the horses disappeared around a bend, he stopped again. I had almost caught my breath when another team passed us. Caleb sped up again. When he lost sight of them, he stopped. With a tight grip on the reins, I bent over my knees to catch my breath. At least we'd made some progress.

"What is it? You don't trust me when we're all alone?" I wheezed into his ear. "Don't think I know the way home?" He laid his ears straight back onto his massive head and squinted at me. "Well, you're right. I haven't a *clue* which way to go."

Despite his ancestors' semisolitary habits in the desert, this donkey had lived his life surrounded by humans, dogs, sheep, and goats, and more recently by as many as fifty horses and ponies. To him, following anyone anywhere trumped abandonment in the woods with his nitwit rider.

Long shadows descended the slope toward us. I looked up and scanned the ridgeline until I spotted the silhouette of Mary Lee and Oscar. They were waiting. To be sure, Oscar was spinning impatiently against the skyline. The sight of them restored hope. I led Caleb over to a boulder and mounted. I shouted, "Mary Lee, call to him!" Most horses don't come to the sound of their names, but Caleb did, at least back at the stable. After a brief hesitation, Mary Lee called in a less-than-enthusiastic voice, "Come on, Caleb."

"Louder!" I shouted.

"Cay-leb, Cay-leb. Come on, Caleb!"

At this, the tired donkey pricked up his ears and trotted up and over the rise to join his teammates. We followed Oscar along the sunny ridgeline.

On the downslope, I caught a glimpse of the parking lot. Oscar and Mary Lee must have seen it, too, as they galloped away to finish the race, perhaps to recoup some tiny piece of their dignity. Because the official time was based on the slowest rider in the team, Mary Lee had long since abandoned any hope of a ribbon, but she seemed eager to end her embarrassing ordeal, and maybe put some distance between herself and her hopeless teammates.

People from Silver Rock yelled Oscar's name and cheered as Mary Lee galloped through the middle of the double row of sawhorses that marked the finish "chute" or "gate." Two minutes later, my charger, who had picked up his pace in imitation of Oscar, slowed again to a saunter.

"Yay! Here comes Caleb!" At the sound of his name, his rabbit ears stood at attention. He sped up to a fast, bouncy trot again. But, instead of aiming for the finish line, he swerved off toward the cheering people in the parking lot.

"Oh no, you don't!" I yelled. "We're passing through the damned gate."

I wrestled Caleb back in line with the chute. Disheartened, he dropped his head and slowed down to a hoof-stubbing shuffle.

"Thirty feet to go!"

The Silver Rock cheering squad urged us on. "Caleb! Caleb!"

I wished they hadn't, because at the sound of all the voices, Caleb veered toward the outside of the sawhorses again. With the last of my strength, I turned him back. "We're almost there! We are finishing, damn it!"

Halfway through the chute, he dropped his nose to the ground to graze on the short grass. I kicked and swung the whip, but he was done.

"It's over." My strength was long gone, and my will had screeched out of town an hour ago. But before I freed my cramped, sore feet from the stirrups, one of the judges heeded the clamor from Caleb's fans and turned back from loading his truck. He strode toward us, no doubt to chew us out for keeping everyone waiting. I lowered my head and waited for his rebuke. Instead, he grabbed the bridle, and a surprised donkey followed the burly stranger through the chute to the finish line. Thunderous applause greeted us.

"We finished!" I said to my donkey's sweaty ears as I tied him to the trailer. Caleb chomped on the grass as I rubbed him down. "You showed them: donkeys can do anything a horse can do."

More or less.

CHAPTER 20

Mayhem in Bethlehem

A MONTH BEFORE CHRISTMAS, Bruce Woolley, a longtime friend, called. "Could my church borrow your donkey for a nativity show?"

Borrow him? I hedged a bit. "He's never done anything in public before." I didn't count the hunter pace, in which all participants knew how to stay out of the way of large, excitable animals.

"Here's how it works. We set the show up in the church parking lot as a series of stages, or tableaux. People drive or walk through a loop in the parking lot carrying audio devices. Taped readings from the Bible are timed for each stopping place. It keeps everyone moving along, so the whole set of scenes is reenacted over and over for each new arrival."

"So what would Caleb do?"

"He'll stand at the scene about 'no room at the inn.' And he'll carry Mary — one of the Sunday-school kids —

to the door of the inn where the innkeeper says, 'There's no room,' and points down the road toward the stable."

"So the donkey just moves a few yards, stops at the inn, moves on toward the stable?"

I tried to picture Caleb in this scenario, with his susceptibility to boredom followed by mischief. Obviously, Bruce hadn't a clue. The more I thought about it, though, the more it seemed like a nice way to help others celebrate the holiday. My own far-flung spiritual journeys tended to veer back to the Christianity of my childhood, especially around Christmas.

Before he hung up, he asked, "Will Joe be able to come, too?"

Whenever Joe came ashore and was far from the thrown-together camaraderie of hardworking sailors and fellow marine scientists, he sometimes seemed lonely. "Absolutely. He'd *love* to come."

On the afternoon of the big event, Joe — whose initial response was "Are you out of your mind?" — agreed to help load the donkey into Silver Rock's trailer. Twenty minutes later we entered the parking lot of Park Evangelical Free Church heralded by Caleb's foghorn blasts, amplified nicely inside the metal trailer. Men setting up traffic cones and spotlights looked up at the commotion. A familiar figure trotted up dressed as one of the three kings. "That must be Caleb!" Bruce's exuberance and hearty welcome overrode my worries for the moment.

When we lowered the ramp and unloaded Caleb, Bruce said, "Oh my. He's a lot bigger than we thought." He led us over to the "inn," a painted plywood wall with an open window and door. They must have labored for weeks constructing and painting the stages, each set about thirty feet apart. Large signs with appropriate biblical quotes were mounted above each scene. The "inn" didn't look sturdy enough to tether the donkey, so either Joe or I would need to hold Caleb's lead rope all evening. Fortunately, someone had thought to place a straw bale outside the door, which the donkey tucked into with obvious relish.

Caleb's arrival set the sheep bleating from their pen, and soon the young calf joined in with a drawn-out, plaintive moo. My donkey jerked his head up at the new sound and brayed a greeting, his voice muffled somewhat by a mouthful of straw. At this, the sheep fled to a corner of their pen, piling on top of each other in a quivering heap.

I left Caleb at the inn with the lead line planted securely in Joe's hand and went inside the church hall to change into my handmade outfit.

Outside, floodlights highlighted each scene, turning them into magical islands floating in an otherwise pitch-dark universe. Caleb didn't seem to be bothered by the bright lights or distracted by little shepherds, angels, and centurions who cast long shadows as they ran to their stations.

"Your turn," I said to Joe. He emerged ten minutes

later looking like an explosion in a sheet factory. He was bedecked in multiple layers of striped material, unlike my single-layer fleece tunic over long underwear. "You look more like the other Joseph in the Bible — the one with the Technicolor dreamcoat!" I said, trying not to laugh.

"I'm the innkeeper for now," he said with a modest smile. He ducked his head and stepped through the doorway.

The church choir posted by a large open fire signaled the start of the events with "O Little Town of Bethlehem." A little girl in a blue robe with a pillow stuffed under it ran up to us.

I smiled at her. "You must be the Virgin Mary." She giggled. "And it looks like you are about to give birth!" She blushed with embarrassment. "Have you ever ridden a horse before?" Having sacrificed safety in the name of authenticity, I had left behind his saddle and bridle. All I had brought was a bosal — a simple knotted rope halter — and a blanket.

"I've been on a pony. Once," she said.

Oh dear. Bringing a semitrained donkey without his safety-control gear might not have been a great idea, after all. I drew Caleb alongside the straw bale and helped the child climb up onto it. I lifted her onto the donkey's back. Thankfully, Caleb didn't trot off but instead focused on demolishing our only mounting aid.

"Okay. All you do is balance in the middle," I said.

Never mind that the one time I had tried bareback riding, Caleb had shrugged me off in seconds. "And you can hold on to his mane." The little girl could barely reach his short bristles without lying on her pillow. I adjusted her robes, which had ridden up to her knees when she mounted, but the sheet stopped well short of her neon-pink-and-silver sneakers. *So much for authenticity*, I thought.

My self-appointed role was to sit on a low stool behind Caleb and hold his halter tight, offer treats, and whisper reassurances when he grew restless. "Stay still; that's the boy."

The roles of innkeeper, Joseph, and Mary rotated every thirty minutes. Whenever the man playing the innkeeper needed a break, Joe appointed himself. He stepped behind the window and, pointing toward the manger, intoned to the teen playing Joseph, "No room at the inn. You'll have to try the stable." Joe, at first shy about speaking up, grew into his role. He couldn't resist adding to his script: "Sorry, we don't take American Express." After the first hour, with the temperature hovering in the low twenties, Joe often had the role to himself, as his would-be replacements dawdled inside over hot cocoas and cider.

For a young donkey to stand still with a wriggling child on his back and floodlights in his face, we were asking a lot. I could tell when he approached his limit: he tossed his head, nudged or nipped me, or pawed the ground. During gaps between arriving walkers or vehicles, I helped Mary

"No Room at the Inn," with Joe playing Joseph (photo by Margaret Winslow)

dismount and led the restless donkey over to another parking lot and trotted alongside him, hoping to settle him.

During a short break, I left Joe holding the rope and went into the church hall to use the bathroom and thaw out. Ten minutes later, I came out to see Caleb wandering among the traffic cones, tripping over the cables. I watched helplessly as he knocked over a floodlight, breaking the lens. Little Mary clung to the donkey's neck in a fetal position. Meanwhile, Joe, now standing in for Joseph, chatted with the current innkeeper, oblivious to the donkey's wandering.

I picked up the rope and pulled Caleb out of the path of a car full of people. I hardly waited for them to pass before I chewed Joe out in front of the innkeeper and Mary.

"You're on your own, kid," he said as he faded into the darkness behind the inn. Fortunately, he couldn't drive away, as both truck and trailer were blocked in by other vehicles.

During the next lull in visitors, I found Joe sitting on a rock wall in the dark. "I'm sorry, Joe. I'm nervous — what with the kids scurrying around behind the scenery. Mary's barely staying aloft. The hard pavement. No helmet." I thanked him profusely for coming along for a rather boring evening in the cold and dark. He nodded as he stood and stepped out of the shadow to assume his role as innkeeper.

With one hour to go, I offered to fetch some hot cider for my freezing companions. No alcohol, I noticed, at this evangelical church. Inside, I tore into the warm bathroom and peeled off four layers of clothing. At that moment I pondered, not for the first time, how males possess a distinct anatomical advantage. Throughout the evening, shepherds and kings alike had ducked backstage to relieve themselves. Caleb, in fact, had already treated a carload of visitors to his masculine style of relieving himself. First, he stretched his legs out behind him and balanced on the tips of his hind hooves. Then his pink-and-gray spotted "apparatus" appeared, roughly two-thirds the length and nearly the thickness of a baseball bat, and he shot gallons of strong-smelling urine onto the pavement right in front of the inn. All the extra straw, cookies, and carrots later produced another "outcome."

"Sorry about that." I smiled ruefully as the pastor's wife hurried over with a shovel and bucket to clear the steaming pile from the inn's doorway. At least *it* was authentic.

During the last break of the evening, as actors rotated in and out of the church hall, I was struggling back into my costume when a heart-stopping shriek sent me careening toward the exit, half-dressed. Mothers darted outside, with me close behind. A feeling of dread dropped like a weight in my stomach. I dashed out to see the Virgin Mary sitting calmly on the donkey's back. I couldn't make sense of the scene. Where were the screams coming from? Just at the corner of the inn in partial shadow, I found the source. An alternate Mary stood nose to nose with my donkey, her finger stuck in his mouth.

I rushed forward, crying out, "Okay, it's okay." It sounded pretty unconvincing, even to my ears. After a few seconds of struggling to loosen Caleb's viselike grip to no avail, I retrieved a handful of dried-apple treats from my pocket. This caught his attention, and he opened his mouth just enough so I could insert my thumb and press down on his tongue. He released poor Mary's finger.

Under a layer of slime and straw, the little girl's finger was bright red and appeared dented, but the skin was unbroken. The girl's mother stepped forward and hurried her child toward the parking lot. The little girl, still in her costume, continued to wail, the pillow slipping from her robe and abandoned on the ground. I called after them, "I'm so sorry. Is she okay? I'll cover the bills. Anything…Bruce has my number…"

Only then did I notice Joe holding the end of the slack lead line. I picked up the rope and jerked it out of his hand, knocking him off-balance. "Caleb needs a break," I said. How could he remain calm, when a small girl was screaming a few feet away? Truthfully, *I* needed to calm down. Caleb had already turned his attention back to the pile of straw. I couldn't think of a single word to say to Joe that wouldn't come out as a shrieking reproach — for not holding the donkey's head on a short lead and for not instructing kids on the proper method of offering a treat to an animal.

All sorts of bleak scenarios ran through my mind: a budding violinist's career ended before it began…a multi-million-dollar lawsuit, the loss of our house…Joe and me living under a bridge, all our worldly possessions piled on Caleb's back.

The show resumed, the traffic moved ahead, and soon afterward our obligation ended. "I hope her finger is okay," I said in a trembling voice as we drove off. "I'll pay the expenses, of course. I hope they don't sue us."

Joe, in his more or less default mode about most everything, said, "I don't think it was a serious injury. No big problem, really."

Two days later a thick envelope from the church appeared in our mailbox. *From the church's attorney?* Inside was a thank-you card with a finger-painted image of a white amoeba with long ears signed by the Sunday-school kids. At the bottom was a message written in an adult hand: "Caleb was the highlight of the whole event. Hope you and he can join us next year."

Somewhat belatedly, I purchased a $1 million liability-insurance policy, specifically for donkey-caused mayhem. At that moment, I realized it would take more than a "blanket" to cover my ass, so to speak.

CHAPTER 21

The Ends of Our Tethers

ALL SPRING I WAS SO IMMERSED in teaching and dodging the escalating indignities that I grew increasingly distracted from Caleb. As I sped away from the college, I said to myself, "I'm about at the end of my tether." Just that day, a terse email had informed me that my once-lost and later-restored computer lab needed to be vacated — again — by the end of the week. With finals less than two weeks away, I begged for a delay. It was denied.

To top it off, I had gotten an email from Joe that morning. His ship was delayed at sea in the South Pacific because of heavy weather and yet another equipment breakdown — all-too-frequent occurrences. His normal three-month shift had ended, but now he wouldn't be home for another month.

All these frustrations brought to mind the mounting battle of wills with the donkey that awaited me twenty-five miles up the road. Since I had no time for trail outings, we had resumed lessons in the ring. After three years of slow but steady improvement, our hard-won achievements — basically turning, stopping, and trotting on command — had deteriorated rapidly over the last several months. Since the winter, I had ridden Caleb only twice a week, sometimes just once. I really needed to just spend time brushing and hugging him, walking and talking. Unfortunately, he reflected my moods perfectly. Lately, on every visit I was set upon by a swirling, biting, kicking, shoving tornado.

I parked the car at the stable and grabbed my riding gear. I had forgotten to stop off for carrots or apples. *Too bad. No bribes or rewards today.* On the way to the barn, a gust of cold wind sent me shivering back to the car in search of warmer clothes. I grabbed my helmet, which I usually donned just before mounting, and a heavy-duty safety vest, which I kept only for trail rides.

At the stall, no head or ears popped up over the gate to greet me. I peered inside. Deep in the early-evening gloom, a pale rump faced me. "What? No friendly snuffle?" I unlatched the top and bottom bolts. Hoping to find solace in his gentle nuzzling, I faced a cold haunch instead. I lost my temper. "Oh no, not today, bud," I warned him. "No playing hard to get."

Caleb looked at me over his flank. His ears were pinned back tight to his head. "So you're in a mood, too," I said. "Well, today I can out-ornery anybody!"

I stepped inside. Lead line in hand, I paused to let my

eyes adjust to the darkness. But before my vision cleared, Caleb spun around and charged me. I hopped back outside his stall and slammed the gate. Snorting like a deranged bull, Caleb rammed his chest hard against it. I leaned with my full weight but couldn't connect the latch.

Fine. I'll just let him win this round. He'll brush past me and scamper around the dressage ring and through the barns. Everyone will yell at me.

The gate swung wide and hit the wall with a bang, not leaving a second for me to jump aside. Unlike previous times, Caleb didn't veer around me or brush my shoulder as he flew past. Instead, he aimed straight for me. I tried to dive out of his way, but he matched my dodges before barreling into me, knocking me to the ground. It was not the first time I'd tripped over my own feet or lost my balance from one of his rough nudges, but I expected him to trot off a few defiant steps and watch me struggle to my feet.

Instead, he kept coming. His front hoof landed on the back of my left calf. The leg felt as if it was bending the wrong way. The other front hoof came down on my right thigh.

"Stop!"

A rear hoof stepped on my ribs. The zipper and Velcro straps on the safety vest burst open. *One, two, three*, I counted. *One more hoof.* My face in the gravel, I hunched my shoulders and braced my hands behind my neck. The fourth hoof flicked the back of my neck and kicked the helmet off my head, breaking the chin strap. I watched helplessly as that most crucial protection bounced across the ground.

Caleb rushed into the middle of the yard and stopped, his agitation visible in the violent swishing of his tail. Maybe he wasn't finished with me. I rolled partway onto my side and reached out to try to grab the helmet. Intense pain shot through my ribs. I couldn't reach it. I paused to catch my breath and stretched for it with the other arm. Helmet back on, I pushed up onto my scraped and bleeding palms and lifted myself onto all fours. The tiniest movement sent sharp pains through my torso and legs.

Watching Caleb carefully, I struggled to stand, but my legs had turned to jelly. I sank to my knees in the dirt. I yelled at some girls passing by, "Stay away from him!" My voice rose to a shriek: "He trampled me!"

I tried to refasten the safety vest, but the zipper and Velcro straps were ripped from their seams. Holding the side of the barn, I staggered to my feet again and inched around the corner. Shaking from head to toe, I sank down onto a mounting block.

Laura was just finishing a lesson nearby. She spotted Caleb and hurried over, grabbed his halter, and led him to his stall. I listened for the scrape and click as Laura latched both the top and bottom bolts of the door before I slumped over and exhaled. She rounded the corner and sat down beside me. She wrapped an arm around my shoulder and said softly, "It's okay, Margie. It will be okay."

"No, it's *not*!" I gulped air. "He tried to kill me!" My heart threatened to beat a hole through my chest.

Laura asked me, "Are you hurt?"

"My ribs, my leg…"

"Stand up and put weight on it." As soon as I did, I swooned from the pain and sat down again. "Sit here while I finish up this lesson." She called to one of the girls to fetch an ice pack. After fifteen minutes, Laura came over and draped a heavy horse blanket over my shoulders. "Are you feeling better?"

I stared at the ground, weeping. I wasn't shaking as much; I could breathe. "A little." But when I tried to say more, tears leaked down my grubby, scraped cheeks. Blood was smeared all over the front of the vest from my scraped palms and cheek. Nothing major was damaged, except my shin and ribs. Nothing visible, that is. Already I could feel my throat closing up, my heart racing. Soon a full-fledged panic attack would dwarf all other concerns.

Laura, a firm believer in putting a rider back in the saddle, said, "Let's lead Caleb out of his stall."

"No way! I'm not going near that animal. He tried to kill me!" My voice came out as a croak. "You didn't see it. Every time I come here, he's worse. This time he came straight at me, ears pinned back, snorting like he didn't know me. All four hooves stomped on me. One, two, three, four!" I stabbed a finger in the air for each count. "It was no accident." The last came out as a sob.

Laura let me blubber on her shoulder.

"I think I need to see a doctor."

"Okay, then. I'll call you later."

I limped to my car. On the way, a fresh wave of terror shook me to my core. If I could have moved faster, I would have jumped in the car and torn down the driveway. As it was, I could barely figure out how to insert the key in the ignition. Just around the corner, I pulled over into a church parking lot and burst out in renewed sobbing.

The next morning, I saw an orthopedist, who suspected I had a hairline fracture and wrote a prescription for painkillers. I hobbled into work; I needed to concentrate all my efforts to finish the semester. Besides the lost computer lab, springtime meant thesis defenses, as well as final exams. I shrugged off questions about the bandages on my hands and cheek. No one, except possibly Laura and the Bridgmans, had understood why I had yearned for a donkey in the first place. I didn't mention anything in my emails to Joe, either. As fond of Caleb as he was, I knew what he would say: "He's already caused you enough grief and expense. And now that he's attacked you…get rid of the damned animal."

Once Caleb realized that I was afraid of him, I was sure he would hurt me again. Maybe hurt someone else at the stable — even a child. In recent months the barn employees had grumbled about Caleb's increasing aggression. I had ignored them. If I didn't get rid of him, Laura would. Sure, she'd wait until I was healed and had time to think, but she had gotten rid of horses for far less. At Silver Rock, safety always came first.

Just like the time I'd been thrown from a horse at the age of twenty, I now developed a genuine phobia. Flashbacks of his hooves grinding me into the dirt gripped my whole being.

During my long career as a field geologist, I had fallen off cliffs and had broken my leg, fractured my knee, and injured my back, so I can say with some authority that the drowning, gasping-for-breath, heart-pounding symptoms of a panic attack are worse. With a panic attack, the rational mind is completely overridden by whatever chemicals produce outright terror. It was like drowning while having a heart attack.

Over the next week, Laura called almost daily, but whenever she asked when I was coming back, I dodged the question. Two weeks later, the semester ended. It was the longest time Caleb and I had been apart since I had brought him to Silver Rock. I couldn't put it off any longer. I drove over to the stable. I would be firm: I would tell Laura that he and I were finished. At this point, I didn't know which scared me the most: his violent outburst, Laura's likely reaction, or the difficult decision I needed to make. Ultimately, it was up to me. My donkey, my responsibility.

As soon as I pulled into the driveway, my heart began to race and I felt dizzy. By the time I found Laura mucking out a stall, my legs barely held my weight. I squeezed out the words through a tight throat: "Can we talk?"

She propped the pitchfork against the wall and said, "Are you ready for a lesson?"

"Are you joking? He knows I'm afraid of him. It's all over."

She cocked her head to the side and said, "You know, he's telling you something."

Not more "horse whispering" bullshit. I broke eye contact and looked at the ground. "Okay. What is he trying to tell me?"

"Well, you haven't been around much these last few months."

"That's true, with my heavy teaching schedule, the long commute, and the problems with the administration, and…"

"Yes, I know all that. You've told me over and over," she said with more than a hint of impatience. "I understand, but Caleb doesn't. All he knows is that he doesn't see you much, and when you're here, you're not *here*. Don't you agree?"

A glimmer of Caleb's point of view — my hectic arrivals, my clothes reeking of stress-induced sweat — overwhelmed me with guilt. How I huffed and cursed under my breath, how the reins slipped through my hands or jerked while my mind with its worries drifted miles away.

"Margie, Caleb understands more than you think he does. He thinks when you fly in here all in a rush that you're mad at him, but he has no idea why. He is telling you he's mad at you because you're mad at *him*."

"I get it, sort of." But I didn't. Not really.

"Next time…" she began, but noted my shaking head and raised hand. She amended her plan to "We'll hand-walk him on a short line until you're ready to ride."

At this pronouncement, my gut flipped. "I don't have time. I've got an appointment." The coward's response. On the way to my car, my mind considered one thing, and one thing only: *there won't be a next time.* At that moment I was never more certain of anything in my life.

This was the worst point in my overextended career to devote time to anyone or anything else. A decade earlier, I had become so burned-out as department chair during a several-year fiscal crisis that I developed mononucleosis *twice* in six months and was diagnosed with chronic fatigue syndrome. I already recognized the early signals of impending disaster: severe fatigue, depression, migraines, and now panic attacks. My whole being cried out for time away from Caleb — time to rest, time to think things through.

My denial of Caleb as a large, muscular beast that needed a firm hand had doomed our relationship from the start. At this stage, I had neither the time, the energy, nor the will to turn things around. I was a fool to even want a donkey, more of a fool to think I could train one. But who would buy or even take a donkey that had harmed someone? I already knew the answer: *no one.*

A few days after my exchange with Laura, I flipped through the latest issue of *The Brayer* and came across an updated ad for Bridgman Stables, which offered a new "boot camp" program to rehabilitate troubled donkeys and mules. By sending Caleb away, I could focus on the upcoming meetings and battles at the college. Maybe I could meet up with Joe in some exotic port and relax on a beach with him.

Over the weekend, I called Lou Bridgman. I hated to tell her that I had failed, but the Bridgmans no doubt had expected it all along. The sound of Lou's slow, gravelly voice on the line comforted me. I edged toward the point of my call: "Caleb's been acting up lately. He, uh, bites and kicks me and others. And, well, he trampled me. What do you think?"

"Well, I know you don't want to hear this," she said. "There's nothing sadder than a ruined donkey. Once they hurt someone, no one will buy them."

I was shocked by her hard tone.

"Heck, no one'll even take them for *free*. Even if you find someone with a pasture and *pay* them to keep them — which, believe me, you will have to — farriers and vets won't touch 'em, either. So their health goes downhill pretty fast."

I sank into my chair. A picture of Caleb on the day we

met, bright-eyed and eager to please, leaped to mind. "Is there anything you can do?"

A metallic rasp came down the line as Lou lit a cigarette. "Thinking about sending him up here for rehab?"

"Yes!"

"We can do that. Farley will work with him."

"Oh, I'd much rather work with you."

Unfortunately, she and Jack would be visiting their other daughter for a month. Farley's method, I well knew, could be described as take-no-prisoners. Yet, if brute force was the only way to get through to Caleb, then it was time to give her free rein.

"Lou, I know you'll tell me the truth. Do you think he is salvageable?"

"Well." She paused. "Maybe. Maybe not."

Despite her cold prognosis, I sagged with relief. Someone capable would take over, and I wouldn't have to deal with Caleb or my fears for a while. Could they turn back the clock so that we could begin again?

Lou had wrapped up the conversation with "The owner must stay away for the whole month. Okay?"

To tell the truth, I wasn't sure I would come up at all. Once Caleb was in their hands, all it would take was a phone call from me and they could sell him for me. That is, if they could tame him again, and if not, maybe they could calm him enough to give him away.

In a lifetime of uphill struggles to become a field

geologist and a tenured professor, all the while tenaciously honing my skills to accomplish impossible tasks, I had never quit. At that moment, I knew what I was going to do: I was giving up.

Whatever made me think that Laura and I could do better than they, the donkey experts, could? I believed that Laura would be delighted, or at least relieved, by this sensible idea. It would free her from worrying about Caleb's dangerous behavior toward me and others. The next day I drove over to the stable and found her in her office. "I've got a great idea. Until my schedule opens up, I can send Caleb upstate to the Bridgmans. They have a 'boot camp' program for problem donkeys."

Laura spun around in her chair. "What's wrong with *my* method? We can do the same thing *right here*." Her response stunned me. "I'll work with him every day."

Laura already worked sixteen hours a day, seven days a week. She had no time to spare. I said, "It's not working."

I recognized my mistake when she strode out the door without another word.

My first impulse when confronted by stronger-minded, confident leaders was to fall into line. That was why I twisted and turned in the breeze at work, unable to stand up for myself. I just couldn't endure the massive anxiety I felt whenever anyone was angry with me.

I ran after her. "Look, the problem, don't you see, is *me*," I said. "It's all my fault."

In the face of her silence, I soldiered on: "The Bridg-mans' specialty is donkeys and mules, you know. They've been training them for decades."

"How long would he be away?" she asked in a calm and casual-sounding voice.

"I think the program lasts four weeks," I said, "but I was thinking of sending him away for the whole summer."

"You know, there's a long waiting list for stalls here," she said in a flat voice.

I stared at her, speechless. In other words, if I removed Caleb, even temporarily, he couldn't come back.

Over the next several days, I cringed at my disloyal behavior. Laura was, after all, the one stable owner in the county who had welcomed us and who believed that a donkey could become a reliable ring and trail companion. She had worked with Caleb and me for three years, despite abundant evidence that we were poor students, to say the least. On the other hand, she had decades of experience teaching *riders* — on already-trained horses. But Caleb was no horse. Nor was he trained. Surely she could see that.

I had already noticed that Laura usually balked at un-welcome suggestions but often came around in a few days. I'd let the idea percolate. Meanwhile I would arrange trans-port for Caleb.

At my lowest point, something occurred to me: if I couldn't bring him back to Silver Rock, the Bridgmans could find him a new home, a better owner. Caleb might flourish with someone who had more time, a steadier temperament, and a stronger will. He deserved a better life. My determination to send him to the Bridgmans bore all the hallmarks of a logical decision. Joe would certainly agree.

Why did my heart feel so hollow?

CHAPTER 22

Tough Love

CALEB PROTESTED LOUDLY enough to turn the heads of fellow drivers as Bonnie O'Hara towed Silver Rock's horse trailer up the thruway. I followed behind with my car, much of the way resisting the tears that kept blurring the view through the windshield.

Earlier that week, I had presented my decision to Laura as a fait accompli: "The Bridgmans say they will work with him. I need to focus on work this summer. I don't have time." Laura had met my announcement with a nod. "I just need to find transport for him." After a minute's hesitation, she volunteered the use of the stable's horse trailer and Bonnie's help if I would pay expenses.

Two contradictory fears had wrestled across my brain during the long drive: that Caleb would perform like a perfect angel and we could turn right around and drive 325 miles back to New York, only to watch him turn on me again; or that he would do his usual — meaning his worst — and prove to the Bridgmans what an incompetent owner I was. Well, that was old news. I was well beyond attempting to save face.

Six hours later, we delivered a trailer-traumatized, sweaty donkey to the farm. It was as muggy there as in New York City. Farley showed us to Caleb's stall before shooing us away with a short "Leave him rest until tomorrow." Not much of a welcome, no offer of a much-hoped-for lite beer on that hot summer afternoon, but no more than I expected.

We stopped off at the nearest café for an early dinner. I'd liked Bonnie the first time I met her when she had helped Laura transport Caleb home that long-ago winter's day. When I got to know her better, I found out that she rescued dogs and horses, one at a time, and nursed them along toward health or at least a comfortable end full of love and affection. In my eyes, Bonnie was the saint of lost causes. I was feeling somewhat lost myself.

I especially liked that her compassion was coupled with a keen sense of humor. If anyone could help reduce my anxiety and pain, Bonnie could.

Over tuna melts and iced tea, I extracted a deck of colored 3 × 5 cards. "Okay. On the pink cards I wrote down behavioral problems that occur in the ring; blue cards for general issues Caleb has with everyone, including staff; green for what I am doing wrong; and yellow, I guess…" In my professional life, categorizing and analyzing rocks came naturally. But Caleb was not a rock.

Bonnie wasn't listening. "Want a beer?" She waved at the waitress.

I dropped the cards onto the tabletop and started to cry. Wiping my nose on a wad of napkins, I said, "I'm afraid he'll try to kill me again."

"So, how will you resolve that?"

I looked out the window as the waitress dropped off the beers. "I dreamed of a gentle trail buddy..." Tears spilled over into my beer as I raised it to my lips. I set down the glass and pressed my eyes against my palms to block the flow.

The bruises and scrapes from his hooves, even two weeks after his assault, forced me to shift in my seat to find a comfortable spot. I swigged the beer and signaled for another round.

I gathered up the cards and wrote on a blank pink card: "He stalks off when I try to mount." On a blue card, I wrote: "He nips and kicks me — hard." I scribbled it out and wrote the same observation onto a green card. When I realized that I couldn't even keep the color codes straight, I flung the pile back down onto the damp tabletop. Anyone could see that I had long since slipped over the edge. Way over. I was losing my grip.

Bonnie placed her hand on top of the soggy cards: "Farley's doing the evaluation tomorrow. She'll know what's what."

"Could you stay for the test? You could watch and write

down anything you see about my posture, et cetera, or about Caleb's reactions. You can use these cards."

"Well, I told Laura I'd return the trailer tomorrow. And it's a six-hour drive."

"I know, but could you just stay an hour and help observe?"

"Okay, I'll write down a few comments."

"Thanks. Anything will help." Her opinion as an instructor at Silver Rock was only one reason why I hoped she could stay longer. Quite frankly, I was afraid to face Farley alone.

The next morning, we pulled into the stable's parking lot, accompanied by the sounds of a deranged orchestra of foghorns and cracked bassoons. "Sounds like Caleb is leading the mules in a sing-along," Bonnie said with a chuckle.

Farley barged out of the house, holding the side of her head, squinting red-eyed into the sunshine. I handed Bonnie the card deck and a pencil.

Farley barely acknowledged us, grumbling, "That goddamn donkey better not make a racket like that every morning. He gets the mules started, too."

As I well knew, Caleb would out-blast the trumpets on Judgment Day. I made no promises. I retrieved my halter, bridle, and light saddle from my car and followed them into the barn. With the halter in one hand and a carrot in the other, I sidled up to the stall gate. Caleb inserted his mug into the straps.

At the grooming station, I groomed and tacked a swirling mass of hooves and teeth. Bonnie looked on from a distance. All my life, when I made a mistake or embarrassed myself in front of people, I tended to become flustered and make even more mistakes. A therapist once pointed out: "If you stumble on the top step, you don't have to throw yourself down the stairs." I sometimes did, anyway. I was already a bundle of nerves and we hadn't even started. With the saddle and bridle in place, Bonnie swatted Caleb's rump all the way to the ring. Just inside, I lined up the mounting block, and we repeated the same old mountain-to-Mohammed nonsense three times before I got into the saddle. Even this most basic step seemed doomed.

Caleb plowed into the center of the ring, where he tipped over a barrel before picking up a cone, which he then used to batter yet another barrel. On the return lap, he deliberately swerved and nearly collided with Bonnie and Farley. He finished up by prancing around the center of the ring, shaking the traffic cone that dangled at a rakish angle from his mouth.

Farley snatched the cone from his mouth and said, "Go around again, this time on the track."

Right. When we reached the far end of the ring, I pulled on the left rein. Instead, the donkey veered hard right, scraping my injured leg against the concrete wall. I shrieked in pain. On the return loop Caleb went straight enough — right toward an open side door. Bonnie grabbed his bridle just in time. "That's enough for today," Farley said.

Struck dumb, I looked at my watch. *Ten minutes? That's it?* I slid off his back and walked him down the ramp. He pranced around at the end of the lead rope and head-butted me all the way back to his stall.

"Life for you, you flaming jackass, is fun, fun, fun," I said, "isn't it?"

After I secured the lock on his stall, I walked Bonnie to the truck. "So, what did you think?" I asked.

"Well, at least Caleb's acting his normal self." She sighed and handed me back the multicolor deck of index cards. "I didn't write anything down. Farley can see what's wrong."

And with that Bonnie hugged me and set off down the road.

I had stowed my bridle and saddle into the trunk of my car and opened the car door when Farley stormed past. "You know what? You're a wimp!" Her roar swept across the parking lot. "That donkey has absolutely *no* respect for you. He walks all over you. And you let him!"

Alone and exposed in the harsh sun, I nearly doubled over in shame. "I don't know what to do," I wailed at her retreating back. The Bridgman family had no doubt expected to see some progress since they had trained Caleb and me three years earlier. Instead, I had brought him back in a last-ditch attempt to save him from the glue factory. I leaned against the car and waited.

Farley reached the back door of the house before turning. "I'll work with him this afternoon," she said in a quieter voice. "Tell you what I think."

"Okay. I'll stop by tomorrow morning before I hit the road." Just as well Farley hadn't offered a lengthy debriefing, because halfway down the road I burst into tears. Without Lou's soothing, gravel-filled voice or Jack's wisecracks to make the hard lessons easier to bear, I couldn't wait to reach the musty motel room, where I could hole up for a good cry.

That evening my department chair called me. Cell coverage had improved since I had last been here. But, given my mood, I wished it hadn't. He announced that the date for his knee-replacement surgery conflicted with a mandatory retreat for senior administrators and department heads. As assistant department chair, I had to attend in his place. All senior staff, up to and including the president and his scheming provost, he said, would be there. Two days of sharing meals and discussions with top officials frightened me, but I had to go.

Putting college-related concerns aside, I ruminated over what Farley would say in the morning. I had asked for the truth but dreaded hearing what I already knew — that not only was I a hopeless rider and trainer but my donkey was now unpredictable, "spoiled" in the worst sense of the word. Therefore, *dangerous*. I still shuddered when I recalled the full weight of each of his granite-hard hooves when he'd trampled me.

Underneath the turmoil I felt about what I was going to hear from Farley, I realized my chest was loosening up. Other, wiser minds would decide his fate. But, at the same time, I reminded myself that it was *his* life that was on the line, not mine. The problem was, Caleb didn't know it.

As I turned into the driveway and parked next to the Bridgmans' barn, I steeled myself to listen to Farley's judgment regarding my donkey's future.

If the verdict was that he had been irreparably harmed, then no one would fault me for getting rid of Caleb now, since he had injured me. I could pretend the whole donkey fiasco was just a three-year bad dream. Or a midlife psychosis. So, I didn't buy a red convertible sports car or a sailboat in midlife but a donkey. Why not?

I rushed inside the barn and up to Caleb's stall to squelch his foghorn greeting before it woke the dead. I strode up the dim aisle to the familiar white nose twitching in anticipation. "I'm sorry, Caleb," I whispered, "but I can't do this anymore." He munched on the carrot I offered, unaware. Or maybe there was something: As soon as I turned my back he started to snuffle softly. Not in his usual boisterous or demanding tone. He sounded sad, as if he sensed I wasn't coming back.

I left the barn and joined Farley and two young men at an outside picnic table. No one offered a breakfast beer, so

I ducked into the cool, dark kitchen and poured myself a cup of coffee.

As soon as I slid onto the picnic bench across from Farley, she slammed her can onto the table. Annoyance seemed to be her default mode, at least in my presence — pissed off alternating with short bouts of *really* pissed off. The gritty red eyes of the humans at the table suggested another reason for their bad moods: too much partying the night before. No one offered any introductions, so I gazed out over the lower pasture, where a light haze promised a steamy day. I let my mind wander to the *Doctor Zhivago* vistas of that winter at Bridgman Stables. It seemed longer than three years ago when I had brimmed with happy dreams about riding across the snowy hills on my new donkey. And we had lived that dream, once.

Not wanting to rush the subject, I listened to their comfortable buzz about the animals, the weather, the price of hay. Without warning, Farley started in, addressing me: "I rode Caleb yesterday evening. Or, I should say, I attempted to ride him. The damn donkey tried to throw me. I gave him good for that, believe me. But he just fought all the more to scrape me off." She shook her head in wonderment. "He's a mess. Bit me real hard and tried to run over one of my students. He's done."

Although his behavior confirmed the worst, still, I was surprised that even Farley couldn't control him. All traces of his former self were gone. Before I could turn away, my eyes filled with tears. The men stood, mumbling something about "things to do."

Farley sipped her beer and sighed. In a softer voice than I had ever heard from her, she said, "I talked to my folks on the phone this morning. You know, we've got some good mules for sale right now. Remington and Winchester. Both proven in shows, easy to handle, well trained. Heck, they're broke to death."

"Yeah," I said into my coffee cup. "I've seen them in the ring. They're magnificent." Huge half-Thoroughbred mules with glossy deep brown coats that young girls steered effortlessly around the ring. But "broke to death" rankled right down to my innermost core.

"We could arrange a good price. Go ahead and ride one of them today."

As I didn't answer, she continued, "We could maybe find someone to take Caleb."

There it was. She echoed what Jack and Lou Bridgman had said at the outset: a green rider required a well-trained animal to ignore her mistakes — in other words, a bomb-proof horse or mule, like the horses Laura used for beginning students. Likewise, an untrained donkey needed an experienced trainer.

I said in a whisper, "Caleb needs a *good* home. He *needs* to be loved."

Farley stubbed out her cigarette and stood. "Up to you."

I looked down at the cream curdling in my stale coffee.

A few yards away, Farley spun around and raised her voice to penetrate my brain fog. "Well, what did you want, huh? A well-trained, safe trail partner? Or a useless, spoiled *pet*?" The last word was spit out like an expletive.

It was the same question she had asked three years ago. I sipped the lukewarm dregs of the bitter coffee and stood, repeating the same sentiments I expressed last time. "Um. I, uh, I wanted both: a trail buddy *and* a pet."

"What do you mean?" Farley rolled her eyes.

"Not a *spoiled* pet. I mean I hoped to learn how to handle him. I hoped he would learn."

I caught myself using the past tense. All during the previous night at the motel, I had attempted to visualize a Caleb-less future. One thing became clear: I didn't want any other horse, mule, or donkey — no matter how well trained. It was Caleb, or I'd give up on the whole idea of owning an equine for good. I didn't even want to ride again.

I stood up and an unexpected wave of energy shot through my veins. It felt like the desperate surge of a drowning person refusing to let go. Farley had reached the entrance of the barn when I shouted at her back, "I don't want to buy another mule or donkey." I paused to catch my breath. "It's Caleb or *nobody*."

CHAPTER 23

A Donkey Speaks Up

DESPITE MY BOLD OUTBURST to Farley, I left Bridgman with a heavy heart. One part of my declaration was clear: I had no interest whatsoever in any other animal, no matter how well trained. What I hadn't decided, though, was whether Caleb and I could be together again. As long as I was clearly nervous in his presence, he would never obey me.

Back in the city, I sat and listened as top administrators presented their new entrepreneurial vision. Not a single speaker addressed the needs of students or even mentioned education. My fellow chairs and senior staff sat quietly, as polite and controversy-averse as ever. *Why doesn't somebody say something?* No one dared rebel openly with this take-no-prisoners administration. Or, were they comatose from decades of broken promises?

On the last day of the conference, a four-by-six-foot poster appeared on an easel next to the podium. Here it was: the new official policy stated as four goals, visible to all in four-inch-high block letters. The college would be administered as an "entrepreneurial center of excellence." The four talking points — impressive sounding yet vague and forgettable — could have been borrowed from the press release from one of those fly-by-night for-profit "universities." The triumphant poster seemed to imply that, if we could just dispose of the pesky students and faculty, the college would operate as smoothly as a business.

I looked beyond our table at the other tired faces. After we returned to the privacy of our offices, I knew we would all do the same thing: wring our hands, grumble, and then resume our struggle to fire up young minds — as long as we still had *classrooms* to *teach* them in.

During the coffee break, our assignment was to discuss with our tablemates how we would implement these marvelous goals. Not whether we thought they were a good idea, mind you. Each table would select a speaker to sum up. At first, I listened as my colleagues mumbled and sighed. *With this resigned bunch, I might as well leave right now.* All my life, like Caleb, I had feinted and dodged to cover my fears, or "turtled" when cornered.

Then something bubbled up inside me. Like the deep-seated volcanoes I taught my students about — those deepest sources of molten rock that produce the most explosive eruptions — I could no longer hold back. Something in me shifted: the conciliatory impulse was knocked aside by a rebellious streak that had always been there. An image of

Caleb sprang to mind: escaping from his stall, kicking up his heels and braying.

"The way the university and its senior colleges are heading is *not* progress," I said to my tablemates. They fidgeted with their coffee mugs and focused on the crumb-covered tabletop. "The administrators are forcing the teachers to forsake the college's true mission! It's not what we're here for." They had heard it all before, said it all before, in the hallways, the lunchroom. I, too, had been resigned, but now their resignation irked me. The energy behind my convictions seemed to come from out of the blue. I couldn't stop.

"If I wanted to make piles of money, I never would have chosen academia," I continued. "We're here for the *students*, damn it, for the love of learning."

I recognized the same weary smiles and cynical smirks I met every day. *That's right. The administration assumes that we're all "broke to death" — too dispirited to muster any resistance.*

But what about me?

My tablemates elected me to give the summary. We hadn't summarized a single thing, mostly just bitched about the loss of classrooms or teaching budgets. My turn to step to the podium came last, and I skirted the administrators' tables nervously, as if threading my way to the guillotine. With the poster right next to me, I froze. The bold talking points blurred into gibberish. I faced over one hundred faculty, administrators, and their assistants, my mind a total blank. The faces stared impassively, some glancing at their watches.

I looked down at the podium, where a bright-red Magic Marker rested in the trough. I grasped it like a talisman. "When I looked at the poster presented today, I was impressed by the clarity and boldness of the college's intentions." I glanced at the huge block letters on a white background. *Bold, all right.* "The administrators have laid out the new goals for the college. Their focus is on entrepreneurship."

The air grew too thick to breathe. I forced myself to exhale slowly. "Enjoined to think like corporate managers, we department chairs must make decisions based on sound economic principles. I agree that this is a great idea." I almost choked on the last two words.

Murmurs emerged from my table. Their frowns seemed to say, "She's parroting the bigwigs to earn points."

"There's just one problem." I paused. *Deep breath in, deep breath out.* I picked up the red marker. "There are two things missing." Though my time, and career, might be running short, I uncapped the marker and wrote in big sloppy loops on the poster board: EDUCATION and STUDENTS. Audible gasps erupted from the administrative assistants who had prepared the poster.

"Thinking like corporate managers, we need to ask ourselves: First of all, who are our customers? At an institution of higher learning, our customers are *students*." I underlined the word on the poster before I turned around. Now the administrators were frowning. "And what is our product? *Education*." Another shaky underline. "That's what the students pay tuition to receive. They come from all over the world to learn what *we* are uniquely able to *teach* them. This is where our focus should remain."

The timid patter of applause that broke out from our table halted when the provost turned to glare at them. Several flipped their ID badges back to front to avoid recognition. Though I dreaded the likely consequences for my department, I left the podium and strode to the back of the room and out the door.

I felt wonderful. And doomed.

CHAPTER 24

A Reckoning

SIX WEEKS LATER on a steamy morning in late August, I headed north toward Bridgman Stables. The month Caleb had spent at "boot camp" had been extended to six weeks. It marked our longest time apart in three sometimes-fraught years together. I needed to decide Caleb's fate in the next two days, as my fall classes started the following week.

The day before I got on the road, to forestall any final decision on Caleb, I had left a message on the Bridgmans' phone to add on yet another two weeks of training. The last time Farley and I had spoken face-to-face, she had declared Caleb "ruined and vicious." So what was left to decide? I could have avoided the long trip altogether simply by telling Farley over the phone to find Caleb another home. But I knew full well that that would be chickening out. I needed to hear her verdict in person. There would probably be papers to sign and his tack to sell or give away. I would need to say goodbye to him.

During Caleb's absence, Laura had wooed me back to riding lessons at Silver Rock. Although it took several calls from her before I showed up, the woman never quit. Once again, I started with old Patches on a lunge line. After three lessons, at least I was no longer trembling and gasping for breath. She soon had me riding other horses — gentle ones, to be sure — without the lunge line. More than anything else, it was Laura's unspoken optimism — or was it determination? — that brought me back twice a week. She recognized and praised the tiniest improvement.

Time spent at Silver Rock around gentle horses and the people who loved them proved a soothing antidote to the nearly nonstop meetings, official and otherwise, about the fate of our own department. If we didn't identify classrooms and labs that could be leased out, others would do it for us. Already the provost, accompanied by a locksmith, had let himself into various labs. When he found one unoccupied lab just a few doors from mine, he seized it. Never mind that it was summer and the professor was on sabbatical. Even full professors like me felt helpless. So much so that people were afraid to go on vacation or to work at home. Instead we had sweated it out in the stuffy, un-air-conditioned rooms, clinging to our spaces like barnacles.

By some unspoken agreement, neither Laura nor I mentioned Caleb. At first, I avoided passing his stall, but when I finally did, the deep chocolate face of a large horse appeared over the gate. The sight took me aback until I noticed that the brass nameplate with CALEB's DREAM engraved on it, though tarnished, was still affixed to the door. But Laura had told me more than once that if I moved Caleb upstate for training, he couldn't return. The nameplate would be removed later. Maybe I would ask to keep it. The thought of removing it, though, brought a wave of despair.

So I was surprised when Laura asked me one day, "How is Caleb doing?" I had to tell her, "I've called Bridgman several times, but no one ever picks up the phone or calls me back." Various dire possibilities had flooded my head: Caleb had died; Farley had shot him for waking her up; he had harmed someone and was sent to the knacker's. Would she do this without bothering to tell me? Farley just might.

As we walked a horse back to his stall, Laura said, "Are you going up to see Caleb?"

"Yeah. I have to go up next weekend. Sign some papers, I assume."

"When you see him, let me know if he's doing better."

I waited for her to continue, but she headed toward the dressage ring at a fast clip. What was she thinking? Something told me to let Laura's thoughts evolve on their own.

The drive to Bridgman provided the space I needed to stow the insane worries about work into the back of my mind. I was feeling almost serene until I steered the car into the farm's gravel drive. Adrenaline instantly shot through my veins. "Calm down," I warned myself. When I opened the car door, I was hit by a blast of heat. I stood in the yard for a few minutes; no sounds of humans or other animals issued from the barn or paddocks.

Over at the picnic table on the shady side of the house, Farley sat with two young men, all sipping beers, almost as if they hadn't moved since I'd last seen them. As usual, no one made note of my arrival, so I sat down at the table uninvited. I got right to the point: "How's Caleb doing?"

Farley flung her hand in the air as if to repel a mosquito. "*Fine*. Just *fine*," she said. "The little kids are riding him, too. Even took him on a trail ride."

"Wow! That's great to hear!" Farley had worked a miracle. My next thought was: *I* was the failure, after all. Of course I was. I already knew it. I slumped on the bench.

Farley tossed her beer can into a barrel and stood up. "Ready?"

I had just driven six hours in the heat with nothing to eat. Yet, hungry as I was, I followed her into the barn. I walked down the silent aisle until I spotted the tips of white ears above the high gate.

"Hi, Caleb. How are you?" I was used to one-sided conversations, but usually Caleb supplied his own snuffles and snorts in response. His silence bothered me. I picked up a halter and rope and unlatched the gate, bracing against his explosive launch, but he moved placidly off to the side. My hands shaking, I slid the halter over his ears and closed the buckle.

"Walk on, Caleb." He followed me to the grooming area, his head down, ears askew. I drew the brush through his short soft summer pelt, all the while watching his ears, tail, and hooves for warnings of impending kicks or bites. He stood still as a statue and stared at the wall. Was he sick? He hadn't been this docile since he had had colic.

Just as I slipped the bridle over his ears, Farley entered the room with a Western bridle. "Put this on. Your rig is hopeless." I wasn't about to argue: just as riders at Bridgman wore cowboy hats and chaps instead of helmets and jodhpurs, their choice of bit seemed to be part of the "Western" look.

Groomed and tacked in record time, the spiritless donkey followed Farley and me up to the ring. Inside, three girls stood in a shady corner near the double-wide door that opened to a slight breeze. Farley surprised me when she said, "First, let the girls ride him."

Loren, a slim, ponytailed teen, mounted Caleb without any problem. On command, he stepped forward. "Whoa," she said in a clear, light voice. He halted. After one perfect circuit of the ring, he returned to the block and stopped, and the girl slid off.

A shorter girl stepped up to the block and climbed aboard. Like a little windup toy, the donkey trotted gamely, no collisions with walls, no crashing into barrels. After two rounds, she dismounted, and an even smaller girl replaced her.

What were they doing to keep Caleb moving, turning, and stopping right on cue? One big difference, of course, was the harsh bit they used. As I well knew, my Myler Comfort Snaffle bit provided no leverage whatsoever. Perhaps a donkey needed this brutal-seeming apparatus, after all. Was this the secret of their success: just a different mouthpiece? No, it was more than that: I was certain that Farley's alpha presence made all the difference.

The smallest rider completed a nice circle and jumped off. Now it was my turn. I took the reins from her and said, "Hi, Caleb." With his head lowered and eyes focused on the ground, he looked a lot like my old outlaw but with the personality removed. With me on board, he moved forward, albeit clipping the corner and passing through the center of the ring. I signaled a left turn and he turned left, but not quite sharp enough, and carried me toward the wall. I jerked on the reins hard to correct him. Suddenly he leaped, all four hooves in the air, as if a wildcat had pounced on his back. He bucked, swerved, ran, and scraped the wall, with me leaning back, yanking on the reins with all my weight, yelling, "Whoa, whoa, damn it!"

Farley shouted, "Loosen the reins!"

The significance of her urgent command slowly filtered into my brain. The Western rig is so harsh that even the slightest tug on the reins causes jaw-squeezing pain. Chastened, I dropped the reins altogether. Caleb trotted around the ring, faster and faster, this time weaving through the barrels, kicking each one aside with a skillfully aimed hind leg. Then, in the center of the ring, he stopped dead. He dropped his head to sniff at something in the sand.

Her reputation as donkey trainer on the line, Farley charged toward us with a long whip. Caleb laid his ears back and dodged behind the nearest fallen barrel, deviating left-right-left, but before Farley swung the whip, he side-stepped and returned to the track.

As soon as she turned her back, Caleb edged off the track and skimmed the wall. I braced for the loud scraping sound from the outside stirrup as it gouged the paint. Farley strode over, her lunge whip poised to strike. Caleb returned to the track and trotted around like a show pony. For a few minutes, anyway. Then, as usual, he veered off again. Near the mounting block, I said, "Whoa," and to my amazement he stopped. I quickly removed my feet from the stirrups, swung a leg over, and slid to the ground. The mount and dismount, at least, were flawless.

Farley stood silhouetted in front of the open doorway, impossible to read. The girls had their hands clamped over their mouths, their squinting eyes betraying their mirth. Farley said, "See you tomorrow."

Caleb and I were out the door when he suddenly became the affectionate head-butting donkey I once knew so well. Alternately pulling and pushing him away, I wrestled him down the long ramp. Outside his stall he rubbed his furry ear against mine and sneezed wet goop in my face.

When he hitched the back of my shirt up, I said, "*No!*" His head jerked up at the unexpected force of my command. I, too, was surprised by the sharpness of my voice. Caleb backed away and lowered his head, abruptly reverting to the dull-eyed zombie I had encountered when I had led him out.

When double bolts on the stall gate separated us, I exhaled and fled the barn. I was faint from hunger and the muggy air, and glad to escape from my latest failure in the ring. At the Warsaw café, with sandwich in hand, a glass of iced tea pressed against my forehead, I ruminated about my dilemma. Our brief lesson that day had proved that Caleb had no intention of changing on my behalf. Indeed, it seemed there was something about me, specifically, that set him off. Of course, part of it was my yanking on the cruel bit, but even with slack reins he hauled me all over the ring, just as he had done on our first lesson. *And our hundredth.* Would two more weeks of training make a big difference? Not likely.

I drove to the motel and flopped onto the bed. Grim reality pointed in only one direction, I knew. Caleb needed a firm, competent rider. And I wasn't it. I drifted off to sleep filled with sadness.

CHAPTER 25

Our True Natures

THE NEXT MORNING I woke up in a tangle of sheets, my cheeks crusty from dried tears. My arms and legs felt almost too heavy to escape the swampy bed. After a quick shower, I dragged myself out the door and drove to the café. Over an egg-and-bacon sandwich, I reviewed my options. The prospect of selling Caleb or giving him away made me sick to the stomach. No sooner had a hazy image of an experienced rider adopting Caleb appeared than it was replaced by a starker image of him abandoned in a field. Yet, if someone could ride him safely when I couldn't, it would be the only rational choice.

The next option wasn't really a choice, as it was out of my control: I could ask Laura if the new calmer, safer Caleb could return to Silver Rock. Not for me to ride, of course, but just to board there. She had warned me, though, about the long waiting list for stalls, and there was already a new horse in Caleb's stall. Anyway, I suspected that she would not allow me to bring a donkey — or any animal — to Silver Rock that I couldn't ride, especially one that had injured someone. My next thought was that Laura knew people with farms nearby that accepted horses.

A compromise solution suddenly sprang to mind. The more I thought about it, the better it sounded. What if I boarded Caleb at Bridgman permanently? He would be in competent hands. The kids, apparently, had no trouble riding him, at least when Farley was present. There were several empty stalls available, and the boarding fee was less than half the price at Silver Rock. More important, compared with the crowded rings and paddocks at Laura's stable and the traffic-choked suburban roads that made riding Caleb so fraught with danger, a quiet, rural setting seemed ideal for him. I could come and visit him once a month or so.

Most important to my troubled mind, Caleb would still be mine.

Now that I had a plan, I felt somewhat energized. I guided the car up out of Warsaw toward the farm. But my mind — now released from one problem — wandered back to the consequences of my outburst at the college. I'd harbored a fantasy that the college powers that be would abandon the plans that would shortchange the students. At the very least, I thought that my colleagues would rally around me with their support. None of that happened. In fact, my department chair chewed me out at a faculty meeting for my "stunt." Somehow he had smoothed over any consequences with the provost. I was afraid I knew how: instead of defending the student-education model and supporting me — or at least putting in some of his own thoughts on education — he no doubt told the administration that I was bonkers. That, I knew, would undercut any effect of my lone effort to speak up for teaching.

The only person my speech seemed to have had an impact on was me. After the conference I felt better about work, about myself. The thought of a different future began to occur to me at odd moments. Could I take early retirement? Right then, I had no time to concentrate on such foggy impulses. Before I returned to New York City to set up my fall teaching schedule and meet with students, there was Caleb's future to consider.

Lost in thought, I missed the turn for the farm and had to double back to the driveway. As soon as I parked, a screen door slammed across the yard, and I turned to see Lou emerging from her kitchen door. "Lou!" I ran over to give her a big hug. I think I surprised both of us with its intensity. "I'm so glad to see you!"

"Same here, girlfriend," Lou drawled. She seized my arm and waved me over to the picnic table. "Go fetch a beer — or coffee — and join us on the terrace."

I fetched a cup of coffee and met up with Lou and Jack in the shade. Not thinking, I kissed him on his sweaty forehead. He recoiled, surprised, then smiled at the unexpected display of affection. When Farley joined us a few minutes later, a chill wind seemed to sweep across the table. Nervous again, I listened as Jack discussed various details about the training of this mule or that with her. Farley scowled at him and looked away, visibly resenting the unasked-for advice.

After a few minutes, Farley signaled to me by standing up and tilting her head toward the barn. We had one more lesson before I left for New York City. The time to discuss boarding Caleb could wait until I had thought out the details a bit more. I followed Farley into the barn and led Caleb from his stall without saying much except a soft hello. He responded by plodding alongside me like the subdued donkey he was with everyone else at Bridgman.

To be sure, Farley's traditional "breaking" method, with strict discipline, harsh reinforcement, and mechanical aids (curb bits with chains and shanks, spurs, and whips), produced rapid compliance. Perhaps the results would be permanent if consistently applied by a determined, strong-armed rider. But I knew that rider was not me.

When I lifted the Western bridle from its peg, Caleb raised his head and looked straight into my eyes. He ground his jaws from side to side.

I imagined the bit in my own mouth. A shiver of revulsion shot through me. If I couldn't control my donkey with a gentle rig, I refused to consider painful alternatives. Never mind that the curb bit with shanks had been used around the world on horses for millennia. Never mind that Caleb resisted me even when the bit and chain dug into his jaw. The bottom line was this: as desperate as I was to gain his respect, I could not, would not, hurt him. I returned Farley's bridle to the peg and trotted outside to my car to fetch the Comfort bit — the one Farley had declared "hopeless."

Right then and there, the irony struck me: weren't we all — Farley, Laura, Sara, and I — attempting to force the donkey to abandon his true nature? Images flashed through my mind: Caleb's expression of innocent surprise after he escaped from his stall or tossed a traffic cone over the fence, his comical acts of rebellion in response to Sara's bullying.

Back at Caleb's side, I lifted my bridle over his head. For once he didn't clench his teeth, one of his endless games of resistance.

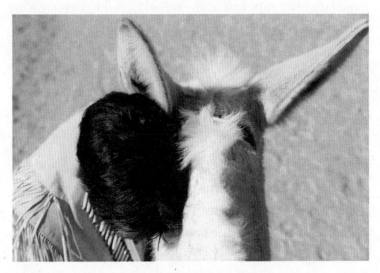

"We've got to work things out!" (photo by Suzanne Vosburg)

Farley waited in the ring. Lucky for me, Caleb stood still as I climbed aboard. We started around the track at a sedate pace.

Farley called out, "Reverse direction and pick up a trot."

I overreacted, as I always did when I was watched by critical eyes, and wrenched Caleb's head around to the left. Instead, he veered right and made a beeline for a pile of disassembled jumps. I lost my grip on the reins as they slid through my already-sweaty hands. All I could do was kick and yell to try to get him to halt, which he did by plunking his front hoof on the top rail of one of the fallen jumps. Farley rushed over with her big whip. "Kick him! Back him up!"

Instead, I released the reins altogether and wiped my hands on my pants. Just as she raised her whip to tap Caleb in the chest, I said, quietly, "No." She hesitated. I looked her straight in the eye and said, "Don't. Let me do this."

Farley noticed the bridle and locked eyes with me. "Fine," she said. She dropped her gaze and stalked out of the ring. As far as she was concerned, we were done.

I slumped in the saddle and watched as Caleb tapped the bar with his hoof. My mind, emptied of hopes and expectations, was blank. Time passed. The shadow of our silhouette grew in length until it resembled Picasso's sketch of Don Quixote. Slowly, slowly, Caleb lifted his head and turned his neck to the side. His dark eye searched my face. He looked around the empty ring and walked toward the perimeter. With no twitch from the reins, no squeeze of my thighs, he traced a precise circuit. Out of the corner of my eye I spotted Lou and Jack at the doorway. They watched silently for a few minutes and then left. When we were alone again, I gathered the reins and straightened my posture, and Caleb's pace picked up. I barely squeezed the right rein and he turned right. "Whoa," I whispered, and he stopped. With just the tiniest squeeze of the reins, I repeated the most basic training exercise: walk-halt transitions.

Caleb was trying to show me something. I had known from the start that I could never win a physical struggle with this animal. But I finally got it: it was the struggle *itself* I couldn't win. I claimed I wanted an equal partner, but in my fear that Caleb would throw me or bolt or do the opposite of what I wanted, what I communicated was "Don't you dare! You'd better not! Oh no, not again, not in front of everybody…" My negative expectations produced the very result I feared.

While my mind considered this new realization, Caleb eased toward the double doors, wide open to let in the summer breeze. He inched slowly through them, as if he didn't want to break the spell. Outside, he hesitated, as if he expected a reprimand or a jerk of the reins. With no restrictions imposed on him, one hoof reached forward, then another, until he had carried me across the overgrown meadow, which was dotted with wildflowers. At the top of the hill, he slowed to a stop, and we both breathed in the tart aromas of goldenrod and Queen Anne's lace. The barn and house lay below in a late-summer haze. *Remember this?* He retraced our long-ago trail ride in the snow. At least the part before he had bolted and slid onto the ice.

After a short pause and having received no guidance from me, Caleb sauntered over to a grove of trees and entered its cool shade. He stepped carefully over fallen branches and muddy pools and passed through the woods, his ears rotating to detect any sound of movement. He continued into a stubbly field of dried cornstalks. His dainty hooves neatly traced the narrow furrows.

I got it. He was saying, "Trust me."

In my professorial role, I had often spouted information gleaned from research into donkeys. One of my favorite ones: Balaam's ass was the only animal, besides the serpent in the Garden of Eden, that spoke in the Bible (Numbers 22:21–38). I especially loved to recount that story not only because the donkey spoke but because she could see and hear the angel when her master, a prophet, could not. Faithfulness tempered by wisdom. That, to me, was a donkey.

Instead of spending hundreds of hours and thousands of dollars in training fees, I should have trusted him. I should have just given him what we both needed all along: time. Time together, just being ourselves. Outside a performance ring, unstructured and unobserved. Didn't my original dream feature walking through the woods with my donkey? The blur of others' expectations, including my own; Laura's; and Farley, Lou, and Jack Bridgman's, plus my competitive instincts and fear of failure, had undermined that dream. All that, combined with the scarcity of woodlands near my home, had conspired to push Caleb and me toward the intense discipline of ring work. In all fairness to Laura, I did begin to warm to the idea of a donkey performing in a show ring alongside horses. And yet, as much as I had persisted in the ring, trying to control this large, independent animal, I had secretly applauded his blithe indifference to commands, and especially his antics. Talk about mixed messages!

Now, no longer worried about the placement of my legs and hands, my posture, or my seat position, I relaxed into his gentle, rocking rhythm. Instead of projecting various fantasies on him — perceiving him as a living stuffed animal, a rescued Third World beast of burden in need of love, a wannabe dressage pony, or a nemesis — I needed to listen. At this thought, I felt a deep inner pang about leaving him at the Bridgmans'. Caleb would no longer be a regular presence in my life. Yet here, he would be in good hands.

Caleb circled the far edge of the field and turned back toward the barn, past the house and picnic table, where Lou was sitting alone bent over a pile of papers. She looked up as we passed by and nodded. I would talk to her about boarding Caleb.

Inside the barn, both of us maintained the same dreamlike state. Caleb arched his head over the stall gate as I closed it. I looked at my watch. I should have gotten on the road an hour ago. I regarded his solemn face as I backed away. "Take it easy, honkey-donk."

CHAPTER 26

An L-Back-Through into a Tight Corner

STILL UNDER THE SPELL of the peaceful ride through the sunny meadow and woods, I ambled toward my car lost in dreamy images. I hadn't even begun to digest all that it meant when Lou called to me from the picnic table on the patio.

"Come on over before you go."

"Here it comes," I whispered. She was about to tell me she had found someone who would adopt Caleb. She thought this was what I wanted — needed — to hear. Wasn't it? I hadn't yet brought up the idea of Caleb boarding with them.

I sat across from her and watched as she wiped ashes off a pile of paper forms. "Lou, I have an idea: how about if Caleb boards here —"

Lou cut me off: "Here, fill this in." She shoved a form across the table.

"What is that?" I lurched back, nearly toppling the picnic bench. It could only be transfer-of-ownership papers.

My vision blurred, and I fought to focus on the heading, which read: "Upstate Donkey and Mule Celebration." It was scheduled for the Sunday after Labor Day in Bath, New York. At the top were spaces for owner's name, mule/donkey's name, and rider's name. At first, I couldn't make sense of it. Was Bath where the Bridgmans would hand Caleb over to a new owner? I wasn't ready for this.

Thrown by Lou's abrupt change of topic, I tried again: "About boarding Caleb here permanently…"

"Fill in the top part." Lou tamped out her cigarette and dropped the butt into her coffee cup. "He's turning into a nice show donkey."

"Caleb?" I struggled to make sense of her words. "Caleb — you think he's ready for a *show*?" As long as Farley, Lou, or one of her students rode him, maybe.

"Time for you two to put it all together, you know," Lou said.

"Wait. By 'you,' do you mean *us*? You mean *I'm* going to ride him?" I asked.

"Why not?" Lou said, as Jack squeezed onto the picnic bench beside her.

The sweet aroma of Kentucky's finest spirits wafted from his coffee cup. He brushed away straw clinging to his shaggy beard and overalls. "You know what? You decided to change. And your donkey's noticing."

How did he know? Had he seen us riding in the field? But this "change" had only just happened. And wasn't

Caleb's message to me that the pressure to perform in front of critical audiences was what had nearly done us both in?

I had attended two donkey-and-mule shows before I had met Caleb and had come away impressed by the high level of ridership. But I get nervous and often freeze when I feel judged. And a semiprofessional show would raise the stakes a hundredfold. "Wait a minute; I don't think —"

"Of course it's a good idea," Lou interrupted. She turned away from me to consult with Farley, who had just plunked down on the bench on the other side of her. They both flipped through the pages of a small book entitled *The North American Saddle Mule Association (NASMA) Official Handbook*. Farley said to her mother, "Okay, I can ride him in some Western events."

She and Lou proceeded to check off several lines. I turned the sheet around, agog at all the checkmarks. "Gee, that's over a dozen events!" I squinted to read the fine print. "*Novice Walk/Trot. Senior Showmanship*. How can a 'novice' also qualify for 'senior' events?"

"You're the novice. The donkey's over five years old, so he's the senior."

"Oh, I see." What a neat reversal of our actual ages. "But what's the difference between *Straight Barrels* and *Cloverleaf Barrels*?" Caleb never met a barrel he didn't knock over.

"It's just steering around them, one way or another, right? You've been doing the same thing in lessons," Lou said.

"Well, sort of." I pictured the piles of broken lumber that had once been jumps and the mangled traffic cones. I stood up and, despite the unseemly hour and the long drive ahead, said, "Have any extra cold beer?"

Farley nodded. "Sure." She leaned over and fished inside a cooler and handed me an icy can.

After a few swigs, I picked up the pencil and filled out the top of the form. On the line for my show animal's name I wrote the fancy one Laura had placed on his nameplate at Silver Rock, which I never used.

Lou read it. "'Caleb's Dream'? That's his full name? Hmmpfh."

"Sounds impressive, though, doesn't it?" I chuckled to hide my embarrassment.

Lou and Farley flashed a glance at each other. "He's a dreamer all right. You both are."

Jack sipped his drink and added, "Caleb watches your every move. He wants to be with you, even if he doesn't understand why you're often mad at him."

That's true, I thought. I was ashamed. It was so obvious.

Lou put the handbook aside, so I slid it toward me and looked inside. It read like a military field manual, packed with mysterious diagrams and terminology, such as *L-Back-Through* and *Diagonal-Sit-Trot*.

"Caleb has never backed up *once* on command, as far as I know, except when I urge him to move *forward*."

Lou and Jack smiled but looked away.

The show was only ten days away, and I was leaving to go back to work. There would be no time to practice. "It's no use. I'm nowhere near ready for this." I dropped the handbook on the table and stood.

Jack said, "Let me tell you something. A donkey will never make you look good. *Never.* He might perform a pattern in the ring perfectly fifty times in a row, and the fifty-first time — right there in the show ring — he'll plant his feet, do the pattern backward, or run out of the ring with a big 'adios.'" Jack threw his head back and laughed at the image. "A donkey thinks perfection is boring."

I had to smile. Me, too, Caleb. Me, too.

As if Jack's comments had settled all doubts, Lou collected the entry form and said, "Okay, then, that adds up to $112. Plus, the trailer fee from here to Bath will be $70."

It was past the time for me, ready or not, to leave for the city. "Well, okay, then. I'll meet you in Bath." I was more than a little bemused by the unexpected turn of events.

Jack stood and patted me on the back and said, "You know what? You kept at it. If any animal can appreciate tenacity, it's a donkey."

My car had just reached the top of the first hill when the penny dropped. *What about after the show? What about boarding Caleb with the Bridgmans permanently?* Giddy and confused as I was about the show, I had never finished asking them about it. I pulled the car over and pulled out my phone, but instead of calling Lou, I dialed the number for Silver Rock Farm. At the message prompt, I said, "Laura, I need to talk to you right away about Caleb."

Unusual for her, she picked right up. "Margie? What —"

"The Bridgmans want Caleb to perform in a show! Can you believe it?" I fairly gushed with news about how well Caleb was doing — as if it was only he who had changed. I ended with, "Do you want to come?"

Laura responded in the neutral tone I most dreaded: "And then what?"

I proceeded with caution. "I don't know. I guess he can board at Bridgman."

"Don't be silly, Margie! What's the date of the show? Let me check my calendar." After a few minutes she came back on the line and said, "Right. Bruce and I can drive up to see the show. That way we can bring him back home that evening."

Home. Just as I had missed Caleb's signals, I had misread Laura's and the Bridgmans', too. Jack's words echoed in my mind: "He wants to be with you." Not some hypothetical perfect owner. With *me.*

I found a spot to turn around and raced back to the farm. No one seemed to be about. Even the dogs were silent. If the Bridgmans saw me return, they would assume I had forgotten something. Well, I had. Something vital.

I ran up to Caleb's stall and watched as he chomped quietly on some hay. I spread my arms over the gate and whispered his name. He came over to the door and dropped his heavy head on my shoulder. I buried my face in his slightly damp neck. Faint traces of summer meadow underlay the musky odor of exertion. This was the scent of his wild, true self that had so stirred me when I first met him. A self that I and others had struggled so mightily to break with bits and whips, spurs and yelling.

Had I really considered giving up his presence in my daily life just because no one had been able to break his spirit? Is that what I really wanted — or strove for myself? A spiritless, docile creature? I pressed my face deeper into his short mane and felt my heart thud.

Caleb stood stock-still for once, as if he wanted to make certain I could hear my own answer. "Caleb," I whispered, "we're going home."

CHAPTER 27

No Chickening Out

THROUGHOUT THE THREE-HUNDRED-MILE drive to Bath, Joe endured my increasingly shrill recitations of NASMA's show rules that I had jotted onto a dozen index cards.

"So, remind me again," Joe said. "Why're you doing this?"

Good question. The last time I had seen Caleb, I had taken a huge leap of faith. When the Bridgmans pressed us to enter a show, it had forced the issue. Perhaps their initial dire forecast and sudden turnaround marked some subtle strategy to push me off the fence. If so, it had worked — both on me and, apparently, on Laura. I patted Joe on the thigh and said, "It will be fine." As if *he* needed reassurance.

Outside the window, the green-and-gold patchwork of small farms flew past in a blur. My heart thudded as I realized that all the most important people involved in Caleb and my sometimes-tumultuous journey together — Laura, Joe, and all three Bridgmans — would be present to witness our success or failure.

At the bottom of the exit ramp for Bath, I spotted a hand-lettered white sign with thick black arrows. "It says, 'Poultry Show.'" *Not "donkey and mule" show?*

We merged into the wake of battered pickup trucks and cars full of cages. There wasn't a single horse trailer in sight. On the north side of town, we turned in at the main gate of the Steuben County fairgrounds under a banner welcoming everyone to the poultry show. I asked a man handing out flyers where the donkey-and-mule show was, and he waved us toward the green wooden barns at the far end of the fairgrounds. Joe inched the car past open reeking stalls full of cackling, honking, screeching, cooing, and cock-a-doodle-doo-ing birds. Some already had ribbons pinned to their cages.

"*Poultry* events?" I said to Joe in mock outrage. "What can those pea-brained birds do? Chicken barrel racing? Duck dressage?"

"You should be the *last* person to criticize people with weird hobbies." Joe winked at me. I smacked his arm, making him laugh.

Behind the dark-green wooden barns I finally spotted a dozen horse trailers. I stuffed the index cards into my pants pocket. In the last stall in the row, super-size white ears poked over the gate. When I opened it and stepped inside the dark, humid stall, I was taken aback by his changed appearance. Though I had given Lou permission to shave his head, neck, ears, and mane for the show, as she had done for the mules, I hated the result on Caleb. The mules looked about the same, if a bit sleeker, when their deep brown skin was exposed. But Caleb's bare skin, shorn of his fluffy white hair, revealed large blotches of pink and gray skin. If I hadn't known that it was normal — I had glimpsed the spots when bathing Caleb — it might have looked like he had some dreadful skin disease. I hugged him anyway and rubbed my nose along his sweaty neck skin.

Joe popped his head in to tell me he was off to scrounge up some breakfast.

"Hold on," I called to my husband, half teasing, "don't spend the whole day looking at chickens, okay?" I hollered after him, "Oh, and check to see if Laura is here and tell her where to find us."

I walked over to Jack Bridgman, who sat on a beach chair sharing Cokes with another elderly gentleman. "Got bourbon right here, and Coke to mix with it." He winked at me. "Got lite beers, too."

Already dizzy from the heat, I said, "Maybe a little later. Thanks, Jack."

I fished the index cards from my pants and headed over to the judge's booth, where Lou Bridgman manned a form-covered registration table. "Hi, Lou. Hot already, isn't it?" I attempted a laid-back tone but failed. "I'm so…" I couldn't finish.

Lou stepped around the table and hugged me. "There's nothing to worry about. We're all friends here." She handed me my show number, a cardboard circle with strings to affix to the saddle. The double-digit numbers suggested dozens of entries, but as I scanned the handful of trailers, I didn't think it would be tough to keep us all straight. In fact, all but four of the dozen or so entrants were mules. And of the four donkeys, two were miniatures, who would not take part in the saddle events.

"Just remember what I told you," she said as she turned away to register a new arrival.

I walked away wondering, *Which one of a hundred things was she referring to?* Only "Make sure you have one clear thought" came to mind. With the clamor of poultry and milling crowds, that would be hard enough to maintain.

On the way back to Caleb's stall, I passed young girls wearing jodhpurs and woolen hunt jackets. Good thing I had borrowed a proper show jacket, blouse, and English saddle from Laura.

A loud tapping and deep electronic hum followed by an earsplitting squeak pierced the sticky atmosphere. An unseasonable chill flashed through me. Next, an announcement I couldn't decipher echoed off the barns.

Unable to stand still, I trotted toward the parking lot to see if Laura had arrived. At the far end of the ring, folks in jeans and cowboy hats sat in lawn chairs near the fence, some with exotic chickens, pheasants, grouse — or whatever — on their laps, which they stroked like kittens. *Oh, great! Just what Caleb and I need: a loud, squabbling audience to distract us!*

Bath Donkey and Mule Show
(photo by Joe Stennett)

The scrap of paper I had cadged from the registration table marked our first event, *English Fitting and Showmanship*, whatever that meant. I fished the relevant index card from my pocket and tried to make sense of my scribbles. Despite the intricate directions and complex diagrams in the NASMA rule book, all the English events involved entering the ring, following the judge's commands, and, at the sound of the buzzer, leaving the ring. "We can do that," I said to Caleb as I led him out.

I used the hitch of a nearby horse trailer as a mounting block and steered Caleb past Jack, who called out, "Give 'em hell, kid!" followed by a wheezy guffaw. Two girls on sleek mules approached the gate at a sedate walk. Caleb shot through the gate and tore off to the far end of the arena, startling the mules.

Through the echoing speakers, the judge called out the first command: "Walk on."

Caleb followed the mules along the rail. I exhaled. *This might not be too bad.* As long as Caleb remembered Farley's training and ignored my nervous twitches. The judge called out: "Halt. Reverse direction. Trot." Caleb picked up a steady trot parallel to the rail, a perfect two lengths behind the next rider. I whispered to him, "You're a champ, Mr. C."

On our third circuit, Caleb sped up and passed the mules. Beneath the narrow bump between his ears, I swore I could read his mind: *Looks like they're heading toward the gate. Me, too. I'm out of here!*

I turned him around and returned to the end of the line. After an eternity of circuits, the judge called: "Canter." *Uh-oh.* We had cantered only a few times at Silver Rock, but I remembered the setup. I turned Caleb's head toward the rail, kicked his inside flank, and whispered, "Canter!"

Instead, he strolled around the ring. Meanwhile, the mules completed a perfect canter in one direction and then in reverse. I was still trying to find Caleb's gas pedal. "Canter, canter, canter!" I cried. Then I remembered the verbal cue for the canter, but my mouth was so dry that the smooching sound came out as "Pf-pf-ppppppf."

Out of the corner of my eye I noticed that the mules had departed the ring. Caleb and I were alone, center stage. "Puh-leeeze canter, Caleb! Phhhhhhh-fpppppppp." With all eyes on us, I kicked and whipped Caleb's flank. He picked up a lively trot but, after a few yards, slowed to a walk again. Then, from all directions I heard a sibilant whisper that grew in volume. People all around the fence line and in the bleachers were puckering and smooching for all they were worth. At the far end of the ring, even the poultry crowd joined in. "*Smoo-ooch*, Caleb. *Smoo-ooch*. Canter, Caleb!"

Next, the loudspeakers crackled on, and Lou broadcast her own deafening "SMMOOOOOOCH!"

Caleb froze to the spot. His radar ears tuned in on the speakers, and he shook his ears like he was ejecting a bee. Mercifully, at that moment the judge called, "Walk."

The mules reentered the ring and lined up in front of the judging stand. The judge handed a slip of paper to Lou, who then passed some ribbons to the ring steward. A voice announced, "In first place, Loren…riding Remington Mule." The girl guided her tall black mule forward a few paces and reached down to accept the blue ribbon from the ring steward.

"In second place, So-and-So riding…" Another girl urged her mule forward and waited for her red ribbon.

"In third place, Margie Winslow riding Caleb's Dream."

Our first ribbon! This was a happy shock, until I realized that third place also meant last place. I clucked and nudged Caleb with "Walk on." He wouldn't budge. I kicked his flanks. "Walk. On." *Nothing.* He had lapsed into power-saver mode. The burly ring steward came over and handed me the yellow ribbon. Not sure where to place it, I stuffed it down the front of my blouse and steered my donkey toward the gate.

As soon as the gate swung open, Caleb headed for it in the nicest, steadiest canter he had ever done. Head held high, he kept up his show-quality canter past trailers and stalls, past Jack — holding his sides, hiccoughing laughter — and onward until we reached the stall. I slid off his back and grabbed his sweaty mug. Caleb perked up his ears, and I looked into his deep, guileless eyes.

"*Now? Now* you can canter?"

The next events at the show — *Adult English Pleasure Class, Novice Walk-Trot,* and *Senior Class* — went by in a fog, blurring together into one hellish ordeal after another. Not showing up wasn't an option, as the loudspeakers' echoes pursued tardy participants all over the fairgrounds. "Rider number 57, rider 57, report to the ring." Each time we entered, I thought, *Let's just get it over with.*

At the end of each event, Caleb bolted through the gate. By that point, I lacked the strength to force him back into the big ring to hear the results. The loudspeaker honked static. "First prize goes to…" I didn't hear the rest. No doubt we were disqualified when we fled the ring.

I cajoled Caleb back to the gate for the next event. For this, the judge, after a few commands to walk and such, simply asked the contestants to back up three steps. Not only did Caleb back up three steps, but he kept backing up all the way across the ring and out the gate, moonwalking the whole way. At the sound of a buzzer I guessed that we were disqualified.

Lunch break came as a welcome relief. With trembling hands, I peeled my cards from inside my blouse, the cardboard reduced to a soggy pulp. The Western events followed, which I hoped would be fun and informal. I pulled out the next 3 × 5 card. Even though I wouldn't be riding — I would hand-walk Caleb in "led" events — I needed to change my clothes, which included borrowing some cowboy boots and donning a cowboy hat. With Caleb safely in his stall, I stripped off the sodden wool hacking jacket and tight black helmet but kept the jodhpurs on.

"Where the hell is Joe?" I fumed to anyone in earshot. *What is it about a damned poultry show that's more entertaining than watching his wife's humiliation in the ring?* Just then, Joe appeared and I snapped at him, "Where the hell have you been?"

"Have the events started yet?" Joe asked me, his eyes wide with innocence.

I was seething inside. "They're a dozen events into the show already, and we've been in six of them."

"Oh, I looked over toward the ring from time to time, but it looked like you and Caleb were just milling around. Like you were just practicing or waiting…" His voice tapered off to an embarrassed cough. "Or something."

He left me to stare at his retreating back as he headed off toward the mesmerizing noises and smells of the poultry barn. I called to him in my most plaintive voice, "Joe, I'm sorry. I'm so nervous. Could you pick up some food and an iced tea?" The food concession was downwind from the donkey-and-mule show, where, unbelievably, the sweet charred aroma of barbecued chicken, the only food available, wafted toward the poultry barns.

As I passed the grandstand on the way to the food stand, Lou waved a dripping drumstick at me and called out, "See that you get some barbecued chicken, Margie."

I had to ask, "Well, at least Caleb and I are trying, right?"

Lou nodded vaguely, her mouth stuffed with chicken. "You know what we always say, don't you?" I waited for some soothing bit of wisdom, but she said, "These," meaning the chicken parts, "are the losers at the poultry show!" She roared at her own joke. I gave up fishing for reassurance and wandered off to find my husband.

A few minutes later, Joe, my faithful, mistreated squire, handed me a cardboard box containing barbecued chicken, boiled potatoes, corn on the cob, and coleslaw. He said, "I'm wondering if a chicken might be a better pet for you." Before I could hit him over the head with a drumstick, he said, "Laura and Bruce are here. They couldn't park near the ring. They're over there." He pointed to a couple sitting on a picnic blanket in front of their horse trailer. Joe and I quickly closed the gap and hugged each one in turn. "How was the drive?"

"We just got here," Bruce said. He and Laura were now married. When he had time off from his job as an economist, he helped out at the stables.

"So you didn't see any of the English events I was in?"

"Not yet," Laura said.

"That's too bad. The afternoon is all Western events, and Farley Bridgman is riding most of them." I was both relieved that they hadn't witnessed Caleb's and my blunders and also a little disappointed.

At that moment, the loudspeaker crackled to life. "Oh hell, the first event is *Led Cloverleaf Barrels*. We're in that one. See you later."

At Caleb's stall, I removed his bridle and replaced it with a halter and long rope. Hobbled by the borrowed cowboy boots, I led Caleb toward the open gate. No one followed us into the ring. "Oh no," I whispered to him, "we're all alone." This realization just about froze me to the spot, but Caleb trotted to the center of the ring, towing me behind him at the end of the tether. At the first barrel, I wondered, *Which way do we circle it? Clockwise or counterclockwise?*

Caleb decided for me. He approached from the right. Alongside the barrel, he stopped dead, and I stopped just in time to avoid colliding with his scrawny rump. Ears a-twitching at full height, eyes wide, he sniffed the top of the barrel and circled it. He stopped to lick the rim, snorting at it.

"Damn it, you know what a barrel is, Caleb." He had knocked over plenty of them, but not this particular barrel with its own unique color and smell. There wasn't one tiny detail of this barrel that he was going to miss. Well, at least he swung his rear around so that we completed one circle, sort of. Clear of the first barrel, I yanked his head up and shoved him hard enough so he shot to the far side of the ring.

"The second barrel! The second one!"

I wrenched Caleb back toward the second barrel — *Is this one clockwise or counterclockwise?* — but he rushed straight at it, veering aside at the last second. Squeezing past, I bumped the barrel with my hip and knocked it over. We circled it anyway — in fact, twice — before I urged him toward the next and last barrel. We were close enough to pass around it — any old which way was fine with me. Instead, he snorted and galloped toward the gate as if a grizzly bear lurked behind the final barrel.

"Oh no, you don't." Finding untapped reserves of strength, I planted my feet until he skidded to a stop. I then dragged him toward the third barrel. *Which side? Right or left? Just do it.* We made a big elliptical loop around it, which he finished with an unscripted victory trot around the ring while my boots plowed a deep furrow in the sand. At the sight of Caleb shooting straight at the gate, the gatekeeper opened it and jumped aside.

I was unable to urge my charger back into the ring, so I waited by the gate for the judge's call, which couldn't take long. As the sole contestants, either we won or we were disqualified. My bet lay on the latter. A young girl came up to us, however, and handed me a blue ribbon. Despite the obvious implications of this prize, we strolled back to the stall together, me with my head in the clouds, both of us nodding at our fans, none of whom lifted their eyes from their beers.

Farley entered the stall. "I'll take the next classes." She used her own show bridle with the vicious-looking Western setup. She swung the leaden Western saddle onto Caleb's back in one graceful motion. When she mounted, I noticed she was wearing short-studded spurs. All standard Western tack, I reminded myself. Caleb chewed on the uncomfortable hunk of metal and tossed his head, tugging on the reins, wrestling Farley for control. Her spurs dug into his soft flanks and he flinched.

Farley rides Caleb (photo by Joe Stennett)

By the time they entered the ring, the donkey's sweaty ears were plastered flat against his skull, and his tail was tucked between his legs. Farley's hat was slightly askew. During the event, he bucked and reared before settling into a lopsided gallop, corkscrewing his body and sidestepping as he continued to fight her. Despite the ongoing struggle, Farley guided him around the barrels and cantered to the edge of the ring. It was over in seconds. The judge's amplified voice boomed: "In first place we have Caleb's Dream ridden by Farley Bridgman." Farley angled the donkey toward the ring steward to accept the blue ribbon.

I applauded with joy and shame. Caleb had performed the moves like a champ. They returned to the ring and performed in several more classes, albeit with a lot of arm wrestling and spurring on Farley's part. With her on board, Caleb beat out three of Bridgman's well-trained mules for red ribbons in the next events and even earned a couple of blue ribbons with real competition. Once Caleb finally submitted, Farley's all-but-flawless performance seemed to underscore her unspoken judgment: Caleb had no respect for me.

Even clearer to me, though, was this: he was one steamed-up, resentful donkey. He would rather suffer the pain of the bit, spurs, and whip than relinquish his own unique way of doing things. At the end of his last event, as if to prove his point, Caleb arched his back and bucked like a bronco, attempting to throw Farley, behavior I had never seen before. A less experienced rider would have been thrown over the fence, but she somehow maintained her seat and aimed him toward the gate.

Outside the ring I held his reins while Farley swung out of the saddle. She stalked off without a word. Caleb, on the other hand, snuffled his complaints all the way to the barn.

"We're all done, big fella," I said and patted him on the shoulder. As we rounded the corner, I saw that a wire coat hanger covered with colorful ribbons jutted from Caleb's stall door. We both peered at the multicolor array, too exhausted to focus. Caleb snatched one of the ribbons and chewed it, thoughtfully. I yanked the soggy ribbon loose and shooed him into his stall. I counted the rosettes. There were fourteen in all: four blue ones for first place; four red for second; the rest yellow, white, and purple. Someone must have hung the ribbons on the wrong door. I looked down the row of stalls to see if there were other racks of ribbons but didn't see any. They must be the combined ribbons of all contestants from Bridgman Stables.

Hanger in hand, I limped over to Jack, still ensconced in his lawn chair. "Jack, do you know who these ribbons belong to?"

"They're yours, of course!" Jack bent and dug a dripping, cool can of beer from the cooler. He handed it to me, laughing. "Didn't I tell you? Donkeys *never* make you look good. *Never*."

I struggled to come up with a droll remark, but words remained trapped inside my dust-clogged mouth. I sipped the cold brew and rubbed the wet can across my forehead.

"Hey, you earned those ribbons," he said. "You came and you tried. What more can you do in life?"

I lingered in front of him. Something had been left unsaid. "I know I did absolutely everything wrong. Everything. Right from the day I bought him, and yet..."

Jack finished my sentence, but not the way I expected: "He forgave you." He extended his hand. "Good luck with him."

Caleb and his ribbons (photo by Joe Stennett)

It was time to go. I pondered his words as I walked back to Caleb's stall. Although he had trampled me, it was *he* who needed to forgive *me* — for years of yelling and flailing at him with my whip and boots, for taking out my frustrations on him, for avoiding him, for sending him away. Yet, after all that, he had given me the greatest gift he could have: his forgiveness. At the same time, Caleb's antics in the ring had reminded me that he was — and would always be — his own unique self.

I opened the latch on the stall and was nearly knocked over when a steamy donkey head rubbed slobber up and down the front of my blouse. "Okay, okay, Caleb. I love you, too!" I clipped on the lead line and said, "Come on, big fella. We're going home."

POSTSCRIPT

Summer 2018

THE SLOW, RHYTHMIC CLIP-CLOP of Caleb's hooves blocks out the roar of cars and trucks racing past only a few feet from my elbow as we walk along side by side. There's no time today to walk to some woods I discovered behind the old psychiatric center, so we stick to the roadside. There's no point in urging Caleb to hurry. He forces me to explore the world at a donkey's pace. Thanks to my recent retirement from teaching and Joe's from sailing the high seas, we're all on Donkey Time.

Since our first donkey-and-mule show, Caleb has appeared in many horse shows, hunter paces, and church pageants. When offered a spot in a trailer, we gladly go along for a trail ride. As a team, we are both older, if not wiser. When it suits him, Caleb remains blithely indifferent to commands. I never know if he will wow the audience with a perfect pattern or play the scene for laughs. Though I respect the rules and try to follow them, nowadays I laugh right along with the crowds. A dedicated prankster at age twenty-one, Caleb still escapes from his stall or paddock and leads the horses and staff on merry chases. Recently, he uprooted an iron gatepost in a paddock and stepped over the fallen gate so that he could join the ponies at a child's birthday party.

I look at my watch. The gate to Silver Rock will close soon. As we turn back, our silhouettes cast long shadows onto the roadway. When he lowers his head to nibble my watch, I recognize the cocky tilt of his head, the twinkle in his eye that precedes mischief.

Before he grabs my sleeve, I say, "Don't even think about it, Mr. Smart Ass."

He backs away, tossing his head, all wide-eyed innocence. I cup his muzzle in my hand and look into those dark brown eyes. "It's almost dinnertime, big fella. Race you back?"

His look says it all: *Race?*

I ruffle his spiky mane. "Just kidding." I drape my arm over his shoulder, and we retrace our slow steps back home.

(Photo by Suzanne Vosburg)

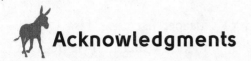

Acknowledgments

WARM THANKS GO TO Brenda Boyle and her family, who raised Caleb from infancy to become the loving and trusting donkey I adopted. Gratitude to the best donkey trainers in the Northeast, Mary Lou, Jack, and Farley Bridgman of Bridgman Stables, who put up with my halting efforts to train Caleb with limitless tolerance.

Laura Butti at Silver Rock traveled almost every step of the journey, from Caleb's journey to his new home at Silver Rock Farm and our first days of training, to my frustration and periods of discouragement, and right through to Caleb's and my renaissance. Her husband, Bruce Mason, provided enormous amounts of enthusiasm and support for the book.

Nonfiction and memoir courses at Gotham Writers Workshop and with Abigail Thomas helped redirect this science writer to creative nonfiction. Mary Carroll Moore at the Hudson Valley Writers Center (HVWC) opened my eyes to the possibility of a deeper narrative. Lisa Ryan-Herndon welcomed this nonfiction writer into Genregals. Valerie Matthews and Camilla Calhoun, whom I met at HVWC, and I formed a pact to finish our books. In two years of multiple revisions, parsing mysterious editors' and agents' comments, we supported each other through the ordeals of open pitch sessions, email queries, rejections, and more revisions. Other readers of early drafts include Noel Barstow, Bev Houghton, and Joe Stennett.

I can't even begin to express my gratitude to the teachers and fellow writers at the International Women's Writing Guild (IWWG). My earliest open mic readings at the IWWG conference about misadventures with Caleb grew into this book. Query, synopsis, and book proposal courses, open pitch sessions, and critique classes, not to mention the enthusiastic support of fellow writers, all prepared this book for its debut. Of the many at IWWG whom I could thank, I want to mention especially Dixie King, Susan Tiberghien, Maureen Murdock, and Judy Huge.

Diane O'Connell, a developmental editor, pointed out where the narrative arc stalled or sagged. Editor and author Lynn Lauber edited the book twice. She saw where the character arc, among other things, could be improved. I thank her especially for advice on which of several beginnings and endings worked best.

I am most grateful to my agent, Regina Ryan, whom I pitched to at IWWG and who turned me down twice before I submitted a manuscript she could represent. Even so, she pushed me through yet another round of revisions to develop themes and to polish the book proposal. I think she sometimes wondered if I had more than a bit of donkey in my genes! In the end she found me a wonderful publisher.

I thank Jason Gardner, executive editor at New World Library (NWL), who recognized the wisdom of the book as well as the humor. The folks at NWL have been wonderful every step of the way. Their enthusiasm carried me through yet more editing and cutting so that the book could really shine. Applause goes to Tracy Cunningham, art director, who designed the cover; and photographer Suzanne Vosburg, who spent three frigid days with a sometimes bored and balky donkey until she succeeded in capturing Caleb's spirit for the cover and author photo. Special appreciation goes to Alexandra Freemon, Kristen Cashman, and Tanya Fox for their sharp eyes and tactful suggestions; and to Monique Muhlenkamp, Munro Magruder, and Ami Parkerson for their publicity, marketing, and sales expertise.

Joe Stennett, my husband, cheerfully accepted his role of long-suffering good sport during many trips to donkey-and-mule shows and holiday pageants, through illnesses and retirement decisions, and throughout the evolution of this book.

And last but not least, without Caleb acting as both mirror and foil, I would never have written this book. He continues as my muse in all creative endeavors. "Walk on with me, Caleb."

Joe, Caleb, and me (photo by Regina Ryan)

About the Author

MARGARET WINSLOW is a field geologist and writer with over thirty years of field experience in Alaska, Chile, Antarctica, and the Dominican Republic. She has written two award-winning travel memoirs about her work, *Over My Head: Journeys in Leaky Boats from the Strait of Magellan to Cape Horn and Beyond* and *The Cusp of Dreadfulness: Fifteen Seasons in Tierra del Fuego and Patagonia*.

She is Professor Emeritus of Earth Sciences at the City College of New York and lives in the lower Hudson valley of New York with her oceanographer husband, Joe Stennett. Caleb and she continue to find opportunities for new misadventures together.

NEW WORLD LIBRARY is dedicated to publishing books and other media that inspire and challenge us to improve the quality of our lives and the world.

We are a socially and environmentally aware company. We recognize that we have an ethical responsibility to our customers, our staff members, and our planet.

We serve our customers by creating the finest publications possible on personal growth, creativity, spirituality, wellness, and other areas of emerging importance. We serve New World Library employees with generous benefits, significant profit sharing, and constant encouragement to pursue their most expansive dreams.

As a member of the Green Press Initiative, we print an increasing number of books with soy-based ink on 100 percent postconsumer-waste recycled paper. Also, we power our offices with solar energy and contribute to non-profit organizations working to make the world a better place for us all.

Our products are available in bookstores everywhere.

www.newworldlibrary.com

At NewWorldLibrary.com you can download our catalog,
subscribe to our e-newsletter, read our blog,
and link to authors' websites, videos, and podcasts.

Find us on Facebook, follow us on Twitter, and watch us on YouTube.

Send your questions and comments our way!
You make it possible for us to do what we love to do.

Phone: 415-884-2100 or 800-972-6657
Catalog requests: Ext. 10 | Orders: Ext. 10 | Fax: 415-884-2199
escort@newworldlibrary.com

NEW WORLD LIBRARY
publishing books that change lives   14 Pamaron Way, Novato, CA 94949